STRANDED ON THE MIDDLE GROUND?

Reflections on circumstances and policies

STRANDED ON THE MIDDLE GROUND?

Reflections on circumstances and policies

The Right Hon Sir Keith Joseph MP

Centre for Policy Studies
London 1976

First published 1976
by Centre for Policy Studies
Wilfred Street London SW1

ISBN 0 9504392 5 8

Printed at the Reprographic Centre, Crawley, Sussex

CONTENTS

FOREWORD

REQUESTS for the full text of some speeches of mine which received mention by press or radio over the past year far exceeded the remaining copies made available by the generosity of the Press Department at Central Office. The Centre has therefore decided to reprint those which evoked most interest at the time, together with some of the source material in the form of end notes.

The year covered, from last autumn to this, has been one of active re-thinking for Conservatives. In calling on the present Government to replace magic by logic, we implicitly pledged ourselves to re-examine in the light of experience and logic our own tenets acquired over the post-war period.

Inflation and its causes are matters on which consensus remains to be achieved, though some progress has been made. During this period official Labour spokesmen tacitly reversed their position and explicitly declared that far from being a lesser evil and antidote to unemployment, inflation is the father and mother of unemployment. Though some die-hard exponents of pseudo-Keynesism – ideas fathered on Keynes after his death – refuse to admit error but go on throwing good money after bad, the intellectual climate is changing and critics of printing-press economics are no longer regarded as a heretical minority, or, worse still, hard-faced men who choose to inflict unemployment and stagnation out of sheer malice or doctrine.

The turnabout was noticeable in the time which elapsed between a speech I made on inflation at Preston in September 1974, at the cost of some opprobrium, and one which I made on the same subject exactly a year later in the same town to draw attention to the change.

But this is only the beginning of wisdom. Keeping monetary continence is necessary but in no way sufficient; monetarism is not enough.* The ills run deep. I argued briefly in my speech *Recovery Without Inflation* to the International Monetary Conference, that many of our troubles stem from the quadruple plague inflicted by the First World War. It seriously undermined people's faith in established rulers and vastly increased the opportunity for socialists to make the old system unworkable even though they patently have nothing better to put in its place. It wasted huge resources, yet generated strong demands for high living standards all round immediately after the end of hostilities. It introduced vast new government controls, proto-socialism, which further weakened the workings of the market and bred yet more controls to offset the side-effects of their fellows.

We are still living with the effects, which call for radical change if we are to reverse the downward spiral. Those effects are now impinging on even wider segments of the population, including those who were for a time shielded from them.

The Norwich speech reproduces the main outline of the talk I have given on the moral case for capitalism to about 25,000 students at some sixty public meetings at universities and polytechnics during the past two years. On four occasions I was shouted down: Glasgow, Sussex, North London Polytechnic, Dundee. But otherwise the case I put on grounds both of freedom and of prosperity and humanity for the market order received an attentive hearing on nearly every occasion and was followed by a lively question time. Also reprinted are two articles on basic issues of our time.

A government needs the understanding and support of the people, the more so if it is to act boldly. We are endeavouring to lay the foundations for this understanding while in opposition. My speeches and articles are part of this endeavour.

I owe thanks to Kenneth Smith of the IEA who arranged the annotation, to Alfred Sherman, of the Centre for Policy Studies, who helped in research and drafting, as well as to colleagues and friends who read drafts.

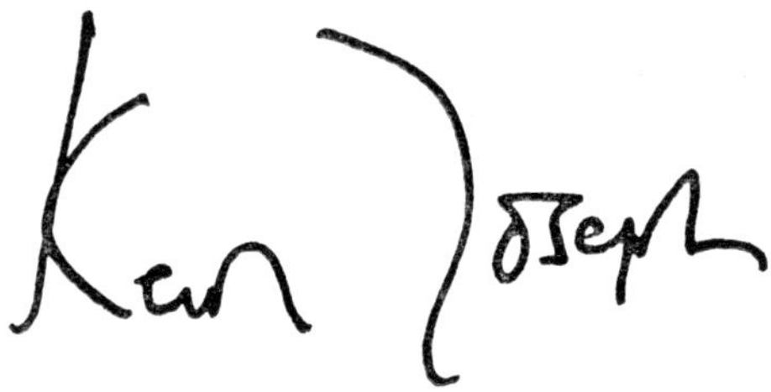

**Monetarism is Not Enough* (Centre for Policy Studies, 1976)

INFLATION: THE CLIMATE OF OPINION IS CHANGING

A YEAR has passed since I spoke last here on the same subject: inflation and unemployment.[1] At the time, you may remember, my speech stirred up not only a fair amount of attention, comment and expressions of agreement, but also a hostile reaction from politicians and commentators. That was one year ago. What has happened since has largely confirmed what I then predicted. I return to the theme because inflation[2] is still the greatest danger to our society and to employment, and because many of our policy-makers and opinion-formers are still blinkered by stereotyped reactions, and denounce those who try to remove their blinkers, as they denounced me then. I return to the theme partly to take the ideas one stage further, and partly to illustrate the dangers of stereotyped responses.

A year ago I argued that inflation was not a natural calamity but government-made, that governments should talk less about 'fighting inflation' and simply stop causing it. I went on to ask why governments, successive governments, had gone on causing inflation when they were against it on principle, claiming to fight it, but causing it to get worse and worse and worse.

I suggested three causes for this apparent paradox. One was misunderstanding of the phenomenon of unemployment and the belief that it could be eliminated almost entirely simply by expanding demand by deficit financing, i.e., creating more purchasing power than the growth in resources warranted, which is bound to create inflationary pressures. The second was the belief that a high rate of growth could be assured simply by this same expedient of expanding domestic demand. The third was the desire to increase spending on the social services regardless of the resources available.

My speech in Preston last September was devoted to the first of these three motives, the belief that full employment, very full employment, could be guaranteed by the government through the simple expedient of expanding domestic demand, irrespective of all other factors, including wage-levels, productivity, mobility of labour, willingness to take the kind of jobs going, willingness to move to new jobs, the profitability of industry, the state of world trade, the efficiency of the economy and all its parts, our competitiveness at home and abroad.

I argued that the idea of making up deficiencies in demand by government deficit-financing, or printing money, as it is called colloquially, is at best for use only in exceptional circumstances and that its use as a cure-all is bound to be self-defeating. Constant use of the inflation drug inevitably weakens the economy, slows down growth, damages the social services, and finally brings about growing unemployment, the very unemployment it was designed to minimise.

I argued at the time that the steps needed to cure inflation would entail some additional unemployment. I added that failure to take these steps in time would not avert unemployment but, on the contrary, would lead to still worse unemployment later on, perhaps without curing the inflation either. This growth in unemployment, I emphasised, was not a prescription but a prediction.

At the time, some people seemed unwilling to make the effort to understand what I and others who long before me had expressed the same views were saying. We who are dubbed 'monetarist' by those who disagree with us do not argue that unemployment would lower or hold down wage levels, or that even if it did so it would be desirable. We do not argue that it is full employment *per se* which causes inflation; we do argue that it is the means adopted by successive governments to achieve a high level of employment which are the cause of inflation. Instead of dealing with the real obstacles to fuller employment which are often very specific, governments try the panacea, the universal healer, excess demand. For a short time it works. But then, as shortages emerge – materials, skilled labour, labour generally, finished goods – prices and imports begin to rise. We have seen it so often.

I argued last year that inflation cannot maintain high levels of employment in any but the shortest term, and that in the longer term, to keep up employment by means of creating excess demand, you need larger and larger doses of the drug, accelerating inflation. In a sense, the argument has since been overtaken by events. With inflation at some 25 per cent per annum and unemployment rising, the price in terms of inflation of trying to use the deficit-finance method of maintaining full employment now daunts all but the most rabid inflationeers.

Some people suggested that I was offering monetary restraint as a cure-all, much as the inflationeers proposed more demand. Nothing could be further from the truth. On the contrary, I argued explicitly:

The monetarist thesis has been caricatured as implying that if we get the flow of money spending right, everything will be right. This is not – repeat, not – my belief. What I believe is that if we we get the money supply wrong, too high or too low, nothing will come right. Monetary control is a pre-essential for everything else we need and want to do; an opportunity to tackle the real problems: labour shortage in one place, unemployed in another; exaggerated expectations; inefficiencies, frictions and distortions; hard-core unemployment; the hundreds of thousands who need training or retraining or persuading to move if they are to have steady, satisfactory jobs; unstable world prices. There is no magic cure for these problems; we have to cope with them as best we can.[3]

In economics there is not and cannot be one cure. Economics is a matter of balance. You must simply deal with one obstacle after another. If the money supply is right, we still have all the other problems to deal with. But if you have too much demand, or too little, nothing else will come right.

At the time, my speech was given coverage at length and was reproduced in full in *The Times.*[4] So one might have hoped that Socialist politicians would at least have read it first, before reacting. But no. They responded vitriolically, keen to think the worst. Mr. Healey, Michael Foot, Harold Wilson, not only attacked my views, rejecting the analysis, the prediction and the policy implications, but also accused me of wanting unemployment, when they should have known better.

Mr. Healey said that I had given: 'A disastrous prescription for a social breakdown on a scale unknown in this country'. He went on to say of me:

We can thank him at least for making the election issue clear. The British people are asked to vote either for a slump and class conflict on an unprecedented scale or for national unity in the fight for full employment and justice.[5]

Mr. Foot accused me of

making a most insidious assault on the full employment theories so widely accepted since 1945. These theories and that commitment, however ineptly and fitfully applied on occasions, have been an incalculable boon to the Western world and especially to us here in Britain. It will take more than Sir Keith's brilliant but twisted logic to convince us that doctrines so beneficial should be cast aside in the present panic.[6]

Further, Mr. Foot, in an interview with *The Times*, called my speech 'misleading' and liable to cause unemployment if put into practice. He said that I had seriously erred in the analysis of the unemployed, on which my monetary theory for combating inflation was based.[7]

I had argued that a high proportion of those on the register at any one time are short-term unemployed, many of them in the process of changing jobs. I had referred to the Ministry's official description of 'the somewhat unenthusiastic attitude to work' of some unemployed, as well as to those who because of some factor of age, personality or physical or mental health find it difficult to hold down permanent employment. I had pointed out that there are, by the Ministry's own explanation, about three times as many vacancies as those notified to Exchanges which are the only ones they publish. If then, I argued, you take into account that only a proportion of the registered unemployed are fit, willing and available for work and have been out of work for more than four weeks and if the jobs available are in fact three times or so more numerous than those vacancies registered and published, then the actual unemployment of the kind which depends on the state of the economy as a whole is only a fraction of the total crude figures.[8]

I stressed a year ago as I have stressed ever since that we should not be content with this state of affairs, but should try to improve employment services, re-training, mobility of labour, rehabilitation, reform of housing policy. It is by tackling these difficult factors that we can make it possible to achieve lower levels of unemployment in good times and in bad.

But Mr. Foot accused me of 'complete misuse of the figures'. And similar attacks were made on the analysis by Labour leaders and even by some Conservatives.

In a television debate with Mr. Foot I warned him that his pledge that a Labour government would increase demand to reduce the then unemployment would result not only in worse inflation but in him presiding over record levels of post-war unemployment. He said in effect that I was talking rubbish.

He reiterated his Government's commitment to full employment policies – last winter's snows – adding that my analysis that inflation must be cured, even at the temporary cost of an increased number of men out of work, made 'no appeal whatsoever' to the Cabinet. What does he say now?

All that was in September 1974, a month before the General Election. What has happened since then? Let us test predictions against events and the words of Socialist politicians against what they have done and what they have subsequently said.

In the first place, as you know, unemployment has been rising substantially. The crude figures have risen quite a lot, and so, therefore, have the net figures. However you interpret the crude figures, one thing is clear beyond dispute: the trend of unemployment is upward, sharply upward.

I point this out, not to say 'I told you so' but to trace Labour's reaction to this. The Wilson Government had to explain it; how do they explain it? They are now saying what I said a year ago and they then denounced:

> Inflation increases unemployment; . . . means industrial collapse and national bankruptcy . . . firms closing down because soaring costs would make it impossible for them to survive . . . jobs lost on a terrifying scale, not only for a few months, but for ever . . . loss of confidence in the pound . . . the attack on inflation is the essential way to check the rise in unemployment

and to avert the threat of millions indefinitely out of work, and young people unable to start their working lives . . .[9]

I am quoting from a recent government publication sent to every home, with Mr. Wilson's picture and facsimile signature on the cover. I am not discussing the measures proposed; as you know, I am critical of them, and of swollen government spending. I am simply drawing your attention to the diagnosis, to what the government is now saying about the relationship between inflation and unemployment.

Not long ago, when we were in office, Labour blamed us for the unemployment and demanded immediate reflation, a euphemism for inflationary deficit financing; spoke as though we could abolish unemployment by an act of will, and as though we refrained from doing so simply out of ill-will towards working people.[10] Now they are resisting similar calls from the trade unions, and rightly so. Even a year ago, when I argued that inflationary deficit financing was not a cure for unemployment in our days but a cause, I was attacked by Labour leaders. I rejoice in their greater wisdom now that they are in government; I hope that it will survive our return to office. I cannot be sure that this will happen, since their present sudden access of understanding cannot be separated from the fact that they have to explain to their own followers why unemployment and unemployment figures have risen so substantially since last October.

In this context, the difference between what Mr. Foot said last September and what his Ministry has since said is instructive. I refer you to the May 1975 issue of the *Department of Employment News*, the Department's internal newspaper. In a front-page article, under the title 'What unemployment figures really mean', and a very good question too, it argues that:

It is important to realise what unemployment figures really mean. And there is one basic fact about them that many people probably fail to realise.

Totally wrong

The idea that the unemployed are a fixed "pool" of people is totally wrong. Very large numbers of people come and go onto the register of the unemployed every month.

About 300,000 adult people join or re-join the register every month and about the same number leave it, usually because they have found new jobs; though, of course, some of those who stay on the register are there for a considerable time.

Recent years

The time spent on the register ranges from less than one day to well over two years, but the *average* length of a completed spell on the register in recent years has been between six and ten weeks.

And a large number of people who are registered as unemployed for long periods are over 60.

The article rightly warns readers to bear these facts in mind when unemployment figures are being talked about. I hope its authors have drawn the attention of their Minister, Mr. Foot, to the article. Does he accept it? We deserve an answer.

For some time, the Socialists have accused us of hard-heartedness, of wanting unemployment as a solution for inflation. Their actions no less than their words have come part of the way towards belying these accusations. For if only ill-will of ravenous Tories were the cause of unemployment, and if governments could reduce it by simple decisions and acts, would the Labour government tolerate the present levels of unemployment for one moment, not to speak of the levels likely to be reached in the near future?

And just because we Conservatives do not, for the most part, wear our hearts on our sleeves, this does not mean that we have any less awareness, sympathy or sense of urgency towards those who through no fault or shortcoming of their own find their world shattered by unemployment. There are very many among the total who are desperately keen to find work but unable to do so. The older man, be he unskilled or skilled – particularly if his particular skills become devalued, the foreman and the executive, are among the worst sufferers. But the fact remains that there are more of these victims today than at any time since the war, after 18 months of Labour rule at that, precisely because of inflationary policies undertaken when real unemployment was a good deal lower than it is today, with the stated aim of lowering it further. In other words, it is precisely because clear-headed analysis was rejected as 'hard hearted', 'wanting unemployment', and all the other epithets wielded by Wilson, Foot, Healey *et al* that increasing numbers of people are undergoing these tragic experiences through no fault of their own.

The Labour leaders owe it to us, to themselves and to the British people to draw conclusions from this sad continuing story. The first conclusion is that there are limits to what government can do, however good their intentions, in the way of ensuring jobs, living standards and other benefits. The limits are set not only by the overall effects of government policies including the side-effects of many policies not immediately directed to employment, but also by world conditions, and by how millions of individuals and groups such as trade unions behave.

Mr. Wilson's broadsheet to the nation goes some way towards recognising this. He argues that if workers insist on demanding more than a reasonable wage under the circumstances, they may price themselves or their fellow workers out of jobs.

There is little any government can do to prevent this, unless it can bring the facts home by word and deed. That is the point. For 25 years or more, we deluded ourselves into believing that governments could prevent excessive wage settlements destroying jobs. We were urged to believe that we could do this simply by increasing demand, by printing money. Mr. Wilson has now explicitly recognised that this is not so. Mr. Healey has implicitly recognised it by his policies. Mr. Benn refuses to admit it at all. Mr. Foot's position is not yet clear.

This should no longer be an issue of contention between the parties. Nor need it be an issue inside the parties. We have had our own problems on this subject inside the Conservative Party, and should not be too coy to admit it. I hope that those who disagree with what I am saying will explain their reasoning as thoroughly as I have tried to explain mine.

Both parties, all parties, must set out from the sad fact that unemployment is getting worse as a result of mistakes made by governments. In the past 18 months the present government has done more than any, I fear, to undermine business confidence and throttle the small and medium businesses which play such an important part in providing employment. But to save employment we must restore business profitability, not try to cure effects while leaving causes untouched.

When we were in office, Labour clamour at a time of lower unemployment than now contributed to pushing us into reflationary measures which set the inflationary spiral off. Labour may have gained some short-term political advantage by their tactics, but their statements and attitudes then are boomeranging on them now. We Conservatives are in no mood to gloat over Labour's difficulties or seek short-term party advantage from them. That kind of behaviour is self-defeating in the longer term, when promises or implied promises fall due for redemption. Moreover, the electorate, the British public, is one of the most mature in the world, blessed with commonsense and observation.

The public know that there are many jobs going, unfilled vacancies, hundreds of thousands of them, all over the country, in hospitals, public transport, factories, shipyards, public utilities, for skilled, unskilled and semi-skilled workers. The public knows that there are problems in changing jobs, taking a job at lower pay than your last, which may not pay so much more net than a family gets when the breadwinner is unemployed, problems in moving, travelling, in lowering your sights for the time being.

The public wants the government to do its best to iron out what problems it can, and provide a framework within which people can help themselves. But it also knows that there are scroungers, unemployables, and people who will not make their share of the effort, who expect the government or their fellow men to do everything for them. They are relatively few, but they cannot be ignored; there is no point in our pretending they do not exist.

It is not a question of passing moral judgement on any section of the unemployed, but that we should take all known facts into account when we come to interpret unemployment statistics and decide economic policies relating to them.

Inso far as the government resists pressures to reflate we shall not exploit their difficulties and do to them as they did to us but, on the contrary, put forward the same arguments as we should do were we in office. This is what I mean by political responsibility and putting the national interests first. Of course, we shall continue to point out that grossly excessive government expenditure is the main cause of inflation. Government spokesmen now argue that to cut government expenditure would cause increased unemployment. That is their old fallacious argument, that increased demand is the cure of unemployment, in disguise. For we now agree that inflation, far from curing unemployment, only makes it worse in due course. And inflation caused by high government expenditure, on whatever object, has exactly the same effect. And money spent on keeping useless jobs, i.e., hidden unemployment, is a particularly wasteful way. There is no logic, no logic at all, in Mr. Wilson excluding inflationary government expenditure from his condemnation of inflation for destroying jobs and pricing us out of world markets. You cannot have it both ways. The government must re-think its position on public spending quite soon, just as it has gone some way in re-thinking and persuading a number of trades union leaders that inflation destroys jobs as well as destroying savings, expectations, plans and a stable society.

This re-appraisal of public spending will need strong nerves, stronger nerves than this government has shown hitherto. But unless Ministers start cutting public expenditure now they will be creating intractable problems for themselves, for the country and for their successors in the near future. For when the upturn in world trade which the Chancellor and the Prime Minister so eagerly await begins and our import prices start to rise again, and our industry starts to rebuild stocks, as it must, and to increase investment, as everyone wants, how will we find the extra resources to meet all these calls when we are already overspending our income by billions of borrowed pounds a year? There is only one way. The Chancellor must make room for the extra spending needed then by cutting public expenditure now. If he does not, there will be a repetition of the rocketing inflation and subsequent unemployment of these last years. But this time it will not be on a base of 9 per cent and about 800,000 registered-unemployed as it was in 1971/72, but on a base that may well be as high as 15-20 per cent inflation and the substantially higher unemployment we are likely to have if present developments are any guide.

The Chancellor knows well that while some public spending cuts can be applied quickly, others take time to come into effect; the time-lags are decisive. If he wants to make room for the upturn he so often talks about, he and his colleagues will have to make decisions soon. And, if they are to be effective, the decisions will need to be based on far more realistic estimates than Mr. Healey has been presenting as the basis for his decisions so far. For example, in Mr. Healey's first budget he predicted that the 1974/75 borrowing requirement would be two and three quarter billion pounds. It turned out to be seven and a half billion. In his fourth budget he predicted that the 1975/76 borrowing requirement would be nine billion. We said that would be nearer twelve – and it looks as if we shall be correct, I fear.

Unless Mr. Healey and his colleagues get public spending under control now, the upturn will be the prelude to much worse inflation which will in turn generate far worse unemployment than we are experiencing now. Cutting public spending will be all the more difficult now that we are suffering from inflation-made unemployment and because of the attitude to public spending that Labour has preached over the years, but do it they must.

In a sense, Autumn 1975 is a turning point because it is a learning point. There is now wider awareness that there are limits to what governments can do, at least in the direction of good. And if governments overstep these limits, whatever their intentions, they will do harm; they are liable to produce the opposite of what they intended. A year ago, when, I argued this here, I was denounced as 'monetarist', a 'self-confessed monetarist', as the *Guardian* put it, and accused of wanting unemployment. Today, Mr. Wilson and Mr. Healey have come closer to my views to judge by their deeds, their words and, not least, by their silences. We are all monetarists now, except for a few die-hard inflationeers who cannot learn from experience or admit mistakes; so the word can vanish from our vocabulary.

Let us agree that however much we may disagree on methods we are equally committed to the high level of employment agreed in the wartime White Paper.[11] Let us criticise policies and their results, by all means, but not impute bad intentions, the desire to see unemployment and suffering.

For our recent history should serve as a reminder that even with the best of intentions we can go sadly astray. There is no absolute guarantee that any government will not do so again. But fair debate and open minded consideration of opposing or novel views is among the best guarantees we have. That must be the moral of my speech here last year, and its aftermath.

Preston
24 September 1975

NOTES

1. 'Inflation is Caused by Governments', *Reversing the Trend* (Barry Rose, 1975).
2. Running at an annual rate of 14 per cent for 1976.
3. *op. cit.*, p. 31.
4. 'Getting to grips with the catastrophic effects of inflation', 6 September 1974.
5. *The Times*, 7 September 1974.
6. *ibid.*,
7. 10 September 1974.
8. J. B. Wood, *How Much Unemployment?*, Institute of Economic Affairs, 1972; *What the Unemployment Figures Really Show* (Centre for Policy Studies, Published quarterly).
9. *Attack on Inflation a Policy for Survival, A Guide to the Government's programme*, HMSO, September 1975.
10. *Hansard*, Cols 997-1112, Unemployment debate, 24 January 1972.
11. Employment Policy, Cmnd 6527, HMSO, 1944.

THE QUEST FOR COMMON GROUND

WHEN I argued at Blackpool against our party's costly obsession with the middle ground in recent years, some commentators asked whether the common ground I proposed was not simply the middle ground with a different guise. My short answer is that middle ground and common ground are not only different, but in some senses diametrically opposite in these days of left-wing orientation. I seek today to amplify this view.

I shall argue that while the middle ground is a compromise between politicians, unrelated to the aspirations of the people, the common ground is common ground with the people and their aspirations. I shall argue further that the middle ground is a guarantee these days of a left-wing ratchet, and that the common ground alone can provide the stable expectations that people of all sorts and all organisations long for.

For it is common ground at least that things are in a bad way in this country. The economy is in crisis, a deeper crisis than most people realise. The unspoken consensus which makes society work is severely eroded. The rule of law is seriously attenuated from both ends by vested interests which use force and intimidation to gain their purposes: and by an ever more powerful and insolent executive. Crime and vandalism have increased to an alarming extent.[1]

We spend more than ever before on education and health, but with results which can please only the most blinkered. We spend more on welfare, without achieving well being, while creating dangerous levels of dependency.[2]

The quality of life, the quality of workmanship, the sense of purpose, the level of debate, of mutual tolerance, have all declined. The emigration of talent and initiative, whose longer term implications are even more serious than is recognised, is a reflection of deeper, and not only economic, discontents. They vote with their feet against egalitarianism and the shabbiness of socialism. For every emigrant of talent and ambition from all classes of the population, skilled workers, technicians and managers as well as scientists, doctors and entrepreneurs, there are many times that number who consider leaving[3] and in the meantime partly withdraw in bitter resignation, internal émigrés, as they are called in the Communist world.

Our international standing, so high at the end of the Second World War, is seriously undermined both by economic weakness and a lowering of resolve to maintain the levels of defence preparedness, material and moral, commensurate with great-power status. That the malaise and poor performance exists, is, as I say, common ground, however wide the disagreement may range over causes and remedies. So is realisation that economic and other shortcomings are inextricably inter-related. I think it should be clear to most of us that these evils and shortcomings did not begin last year, or in 1970, or even ten years ago. No, the process began further back, but has become increasingly visible because its effects are cumulative.

As I look back, and endeavour to distinguish between cause and effect, between ills and their symptoms, I am struck by two salient features. One is the declining rationality both in our society's workings and in policy-making and discussions, the other is our own party's obsession with the middle ground in politics, to which we clung all the closer the more obviously untenable it became.

You will note that I place our other ills: excessive government usurpation of power and resources, unsuccessful economic policies, union obstruction of economic progress, nihilistic left-wing influence over thought and education, on lower rungs in the hierarchy of cause and effect. I shall explain why later in this talk. But first let me stress, our obsession with the middle ground has been the key, for it decided not only what we did and refrained from doing, but also to an increasing extent what we said and refrained from saying, indeed what we thought and refrained from thinking.

In retrospect, it is clear that the middle ground was not a secure base, but a slippery slope to socialism and state control, whose present results even socialists now disown. Of course, we did not see it that way at the time. The middle ground gambit was accepted by us, the vast majority of us, as the apex of political sophistication. By locating and holding the middle ground, we were enjoined to believe, we should be guaranteed power in perpetuity. And if, by any mischance, we should lose office briefly, this would only be because Labour had been even more finely discriminating in locating the middle ground and more self-denyingly skilful in seizing it: hence, we thought, they could be relied on to act moderately.[4]

Events have patently not followed this scenario, nor was there any real chance of it working.

For the middle ground was not rooted in the way of life, thought and work of the British people, not related to any vision of society, or attitude of mind, or philosophy of political action. It was simply the lowest common denominator obtained from a calculus of assumed electoral expediency, defined not by reference to popular feeling but by splitting the difference between Labour's position and the Conservatives! But Labour's position, as we know, is itself arrived at by splitting the difference between their left and their centre. So, the middle ground, at any given time, was fixed in relation to the Labour left and the Conservative centre. In other words, it was dictated by the extremists of the left.

Now since the left-wing always takes the *status quo* as its point of departure, it follows that the more the middle ground moved to the left, the further the left pitched their own demands, so the middle ground would shift yet once more. First the Labour party and unions would move left under pressure from their extremes. Then the Conservatives in turn would edge along towards them to remain on the mystical middle.

Nor was the Labour party centre necessarily the reluctant victim of its own extremists. Though we tend to divide labour into extremists and moderates, we may well ask whether 'moderate socialism' is not a contradiction in terms, and whether we should not be better served by one of the Socialists' own pairs of antitheses: *maximalists* and *minimalists*. In other words, the difference is less one of objectives than of speed and tactics.

Had we been more resolute in opposing the leftward drift, the Labour centre would not have been so easily moved leftwards. As things worked out, with the socialists of nearly all shades committed to moving towards their promised land at whatever rate seemed practicable, while we Conservatives were basically reconciled to the *status quo* as of that moment, it was inevitable that the party pendulum should be replaced by the ratchet. When the Socialists were in power they moved it forward as fast as they considered politic; when we were in office, we either kept things as they were, or let them move on under their own momentum, e.g., the Price Code and Industry Act.

This built-in political list to the left was strongly reinforced by the actual workings of post-war socialism. Paradoxically, socialism advanced thanks to its own failures, not by successes. The post-war settlement, sketched out in the war-time coalition and realised by Attlee as the mixed economy, promised great benefits while simultaneously, as I shall explain, making them impossible to fulfil. This is partly what I meant by a declining level of rationality. It dates back, I think to the euphoria of war-time victory which generated the belief that governments were all-powerful, that with good will governments could repeal the laws of economics. The belief was epitomised by the late

Hugh Dalton's claim that 'pounds, shillings and pence no longer matter.'[5]

The Socialists made great play of their claim that planning would be superior to the apparent chaos of the market economy, that government would take a broader, longer more comprehensive view. But in practice, increasing government power and ownership exercised by politicians and bureaucrats came to mean the increasing subordination of economic considerations to political expediency, the long-term to the short-term, the comprehensive to the particular interest.

Nationalization was advocated, in the first place, on a number of disparate and mutually contradictory grounds. One was that profits should go to the people instead of to the shareholders, envisaged as the idle rich. But this generalized objective conflicted with the shorter-term particularist interest of the powerful unions in contracting branches of the economy. So the real thrust of nationalization was devoted to the interests of producers rather than consumers.

The public sector, including central and local government, and more accurately named the state-sector, or wealth-eating sector; was bound to spread like bindweed at the expense of the non-state sector, the wealth-creating sector, strangling and threatening to destroy what it grew upon. It took up a disproportionate share of investment capital, scientists, and technologists, starving the private firms on which we depend for wealth and exports. It employed many more workers than needed, leaving labour-shortages in other parts of the economy and infecting many segments of the private sector with its tendency to overman. It paid above the odds in terms of productivity, at taxpayers' expense, thereby forcing up wages and expectations in the private sector. This impinged partly on prices, partly on profitability. The duty imposed on itself by the state to maintain full employment was partly fulfilled by subsidizing inefficiency and technological obsolescence – whether generated by unions' refusal to come to terms with labour-saving investment, or by any other cause. The infection spread from the state sector to segment after segment throughout the economy.

Declining profits, unwillingness of unions to accept labour-saving technology, patchy management-quality, and the unpredictability and apprehensions generated by capricious and changeable government intervention, all undermined the level of investment. This, in turn, stunted economic growth, the creation of new well-paid employment and the higher incomes and state spending needed to meet the very high expectations which we politicians had created with our usual mixture of good intentions and political calculation.

This sluggishness in growth and employment set up interlocking vicious circles. Governments were naturally concerned so they sought ways of stimulating investment, growth and employment. But we were inhibited from looking into the true causes of this sluggishness: the excessive state expenditure, the nature of nationalization and job-subsidization, decreasing returns to exaggerated expectations. The socialists were inhibited because it was their creation. We were inhibited because we had accepted these policies as the middle ground, so that to criticise them would be regarded as 'immoderate', 'right-wing', 'breaking the consensus', 'trying to turn the clock back', in short unthinkable, taboo.

So, instead of remedying the causes, we tried to suppress symptoms. As you know, it became fashionable to argue that if only we raised effective demand by government expenditure and money creation, growth and fuller employment could be achieved.[6] And, as you know, this fallacy was sanctified in the name of Maynard Keynes, on the basis of his prescriptions for the 1930s. More percipient souls who pointed out that you cannot create wealth by printing money were derided as 'monetarists', and accused of desiring unemployment and stagnation.

The pseudo-Keynesians believed, some still believe in face of logic and experience alike, that they could prevent their inflationary policies creating inflation simply by suppressing symptoms through demand management, and wage and price controls.

Predictably, inflationary demand together with all the distortions created by suppressed inflation and arbitrary demand-management generated 'go-stop', stagflation and our present super-inflationary recession; with still worse to come if we do not change our ways.

But inflation and high taxation, and economic weakness did not prevent governments increasing public spending, which could only be financed by borrowing, since the limits of taxable capacity, private and corporate, had already been passed.

Our ills were compounded by a muddled attitude towards employment, which we think of mainly in terms of unemployment.

Privately, the more reasonable socialists have been willing to admit that the ways of presenting statistics overstate the real availability of labour and understate the vacancies. Privately, they would admit that a considerable proportion of the residual longer-term unemployed are social problems rather than economic ones, and that encouragement of mobility of labour, changed housing policies, changed benefit provisions – and not the creation of additional monetary demand – are the real answer. But understandably few of them wished to be the first to break the consensus *a fortiori*, so long as we shirked doing so.

Some socialists, the less reasonable, have for the past 20 years simultaneously claimed that there was high unemployment, and hence demanded subsidization of jobs and inflationary demand creation to remedy it on the one hand, while adducing the actual labour shortage created by over-manning and reduced mobility of labour as justification for immigration on the other.

I have traced the self-defeating nature of middle ground politics in a period of socialist orientation in macro-economic and industrial policy. It worked in much the same way in other fields: for example, housing and education.

Housing is an area where government intervention to cure symptoms has been conventional wisdom for decades. Rent control, the borough bulldozer, and council housing became established and sanctified as part of the middle ground consensus. But, of course, rent control, demolition, and council housing were bound to make the housing situation worse, destroying whatever relatively low cost housing remained, intensifying homelessness and high housing costs, increasing the numbers of those who looked to the state for help. But the deteriorating situation thus caused has been used as a reason for intensifying the very expedients which created it, so rent control, council housing and now security of tenure, have been extended still further,[7] predictably increasing the very shortages and high costs which were adduced in their justification. That the counter-productive effects of rent controls visibly caused homelessness were exemplified by Mr. Crosland's cynical action last year based exclusively on short-term political gain. Yet we were dragged along in his wake by our middle-ground obsession.

There are other social and moral dimensions of council housing which have wrought harm to the social fabric, I shall return to them on another occasion.

Needless to say, by increasing the numbers of council tenants and protected tenants we increased the weight of political pressures for anti-economic policies. So the gap between controlled and economic rents grew, and the subsidy element in council rents increased, putting economic solutions further away and creating increased pressures for yet more council housing and further extension of controls. This illustrates once more the self-defeating character of the middle ground approach.

These developments are causally related to the deterioration in our defence provisions, law and order, personal safety, levels of of behaviour, freedom from fear. Over-government has produced under-government. So many resources are wasted, there are insufficient left to meet government's basic obligations.

As I have explained we were constrained by our middle ground mentality not only to follow policies which I now see with hindsight were bound to create the situation we today find ourselves in, but also to argue in justification of them, or at least not argue against them. Yet the further we were driven along our rake's progress, and the more our middle ground strategy swept us down towards the abyss, the greater the corresponding gap between the remedies we were obliged to justify on the one hand, and the realities of the situation on the other. Hence, almost any economic or social analysis based on cause and effect came to be at odds with our middle ground policies and was denounced as doctrinaire.

So while many socialists argue, with varying degrees of inner conviction, that this is a crisis of capitalism to which the solution is socialism,[8] we remained stranded on the middle ground, the unworkable *status quo* of our own making. Instead of seeking firmer ground, we have insisted against our own instincts that we should somehow find a way of making the *status quo* work, and ruled out the search for workable alternatives.

So, our credibility and inner conviction have been eroded, while the ratchet moved on by default.

In short, the middle ground turned out to be like the will-o'-the-wisp, the light which flickers over marshlands by night beguiling the weary traveller; as he moves towards it, the currents of air he sets up by his movement send it dancing away from him, and he goes on following, stumbling deeper and deeper into the mire.

To sum up what I have said so far, the middle ground moved continually to the left by its own internal dynamic. It created not prosperity but crisis. Far from saving the private sector, it has gone a long way towards destroying it. Far from achieving social harmony and strengthening the centre, it has created resentments and conflict, has moved the centre of gravity of the whole labour movement to the left, strengthening the left-wing, the irreconcilables, the revolutionaries. Because we Conservatives became identified with the shifting middle ground, we were inhibited from fighting a vigorous battle of ideas; we became identified with an unworkable *status quo*; we therefore allowed the crisis of British socialism to be presented as the crisis of capitalism by default.

We were motivated by the desire to maintain stability at all costs. But stability can be won only by riding the waves, not by drifting with them. Stability entails controlling events, not surrendering to them. So by sacrificing our ideas, our instincts, our better judgement, to the quest for stability, we ended by sacrificing stability to convenience.

And the pity of it all is that the middle ground consensus stereotype did not even represent what a majority of people really thought at all. The middle ground is only middle as between politicians: it is an ephemeral political compromise. It has no link with achieving the aspirations of the people. The people were far closer to Conservative instincts on many issues. But because we ceased to fight the battle of ideas, and told the public instead what we thought they wanted to hear, we tended to hear what we were saying, rather than what they were saying. In the absence of our dialogue with the people based on what all concerned really believed, our picture of the middle ground consensus all too easily became what the communications media were saying, rather than what the public felt. Its location came to be determined by reference to the *Observer, Guardian, The Times* and *Granada TV.* The quality media in turn, played back what they heard from us, so the spiral fed on itself, destroying our own freedom of manoeuvre.

So where do we go from here? In the first place, we must analyse frankly the developments of the whole post-war settlement, as it grinds into a dead end. There is a difference between policy-making and analysis. Our policies, whether we are in opposition or government, must rightly be constrained by public feelings, by current views. But our analysis and presentation of the problems, and our advocacy of all policy options must tell the public the truth as we see it, not what we think they wish to hear. Analysis should be in advance of policies, for whereas policies must be circumscribed by what is politically possible at any given moment, what is politically possible is in turn determined over time by the climate of opinion among other factors.

The climate of opinion, in turn, is shaped by the battle of ideas and by experience. If socialists, irrespective of their place in the spectrum, press their views vigorously, while we defer to what we believe to be the middle ground consensus, we lose the opportunity to achieve a more congenial climate for what will need doing in the future.

I agree that the climate is also shaped by events, by experience no less than by ideas. This is true, but not the whole truth. For people experience events from a particular angle, and see them to some extent indirectly, through the prism of their viewpoint, which is shaped by opinion formers, who include politicians, communications media and teachers. Almost any event is susceptible to disparate explanations, often to wholly contradictory ones. So the truest case needs active arguing at every opportunity in every dimension if experience is to teach the right lessons.

Clearly, our views on policy differ substantially from those of socialists. But our withdrawal from the middle ground does not mean polarisation, violent pendulum swings in economic policy as is claimed by 'middle ground men' among Conservatives, particularly those who believe that proportional representation culminating in a coalition will bring social and economic salvation. Indeed, there are good reasons for believing that proportional representation would be more likely to increase instability rather than diminish it, though I shall not go further into that matter here.

In this context, what counts is that whatever the electoral system employed, basically there is not sufficient common ground between the parties to make coalition possible. Indeed, for the two-party system, or any party system offering real and continual choice, to work at all there needs to be a substantial measure of common ground between the parties. If there is insufficient common ground between them, the two party system becomes increasingly unworkable. Not only do the parties have such different purposes that the actions of one party can make permanently unattainable the purposes of the other, but the total lack of continuity and predictability paralyses decision making by individuals, families, enterprises, charities and so forth ,who are denied the stable expectations needed if they are to function effectively.

I suggest that in recent years, the measure of common ground between the parties has been eroded dangerously, mainly because of the leftward lurch of the centre of gravity of the Labour movement, which came about as I have argued, as a result of our middle ground fixation. In consequence, it has become increasingly difficult to make the two party system work. We urgently need to restore this measure of common ground. Without it many of our democratic constitutional and economic aspirations are at risk. So long as we have still to achieve this measure of common ground, it is idle to talk about coalition, which needs a far wider measure of common ground to make it workable. But if we had sufficiently wide common ground to make our party system, our constitutional and legal and economic arrangements work adequately, then hankering for a coalition government would cease anyway.

Now from what I have said earlier it follows that our Conservative obsession with the middle ground shares responsibility for the erosion of the common ground between the parties. How are we to restore it? First, we must make it clear where we stand. I distinguish here between the descending hierarchies: values, aspiration, understanding, policies. I also distinguish between voters and party supporters on the one hand, and those who set the tone of a party in Parliament, unions and the country, on the other. I distinguish between politicians proper, be they MPs or union leaders, and the many people associated with parties – academics, journalists, writers, managers, professional men and other groups and circles who, though they have a party orientation, regard the party as a means to an end and are prepared to judge policies by results, not just by their authorship.

Let me begin with the people's values and aspirations. Our task is to articulate them, to compare them with present realities and possibilities and to bring out the implications for policy. Aspirations, however, desirable, may conflict one with another. If you make welfare more freely available and less selective, exercising the instinct of compassion, how does that impinge on taxes levied on the many, the readiness to work of the few, the public mood, the level of responsibility, the scope for prosperity? The aspiration that all should be well housed is wholly admirable.

But does it follow that rent control and security of tenure will help achieve the objective? We all favour economic growth, steady prices, a predictable framework within which people can plan their lives and their work. When we oppose the extension of state control, it is because experience has demonstrated that far from achieving greater stability it is a de-stabilising factor.

There has been a shift, true, in what was expected from government. Until recently, government was expected to confine its role to setting the framework within which people would be free to pursue their own mixture of self-interest and altruism, with a safety net for the failures from whatever cause. Within this framework people would make their decisions, great and small, and take the consequences, confident that the rug would not be pulled from under their feet, and that if government had any role at all, it would be a stabilizing one. The second World War brought about a swing of the pendulum in which it came to be believed that government could do almost everything for everybody without infringing freedom or opportunity. Party competition to offer 'more to everybody' bid up this process. We ignored the interaction between these two conflicting roles of government: the regulatory function and the pseudo-entrepreneurial, the job of holding the ring, and participation. But I think public opinion has already grown wise, or at least wiser, to the limits of what government can do for people, to the decreasing returns and counter-productive nature of government provision and intervention beyond a certain point. The public, I believe, would welcome a return to the conception of government not as the all-powerful managers of our lives, but as the framework within which we run our own lives.

I repeat that in contrast to the middle ground, which is a compromise between politicians and between policies, the common ground is what can be shared by politicians with the people. We share more values and aspirations with the people, however they vote, than we share understanding and policies. The difference is particularly wide at present.

We all read and see the same news, so it follows too that we have more in common with the people in our shared picture of the factual position than in our analysis of the causes and less still in our conclusions as to what ought to be done.

As to the measure of common ground we can share with non-conservative politicians, this will vary not only according to their place in the perceived political spectrum, though labels are often too simplistic, but also to their degree of commitment to party and creed. It is not our job to seek common ground with one particular group in the Labour movement, but to explore what common ground exists between us and any groups in the movement and its supporters. We should beware of accepting any simple dichotomy of 'right-left', 'moderate-extreme', but should treat socialists as we find them.[9]

It should be easier to explore common ground now that the crisis is shaking the cocksureness of many Labour supporters, who – among others – had accepted much of the post war settlement as the natural and irreversible order of things. We seek to persuade large numbers of them that insofar as our objectives are the same as theirs, our understanding and policies, though different from theirs, deserve not only open-minded consideration, since socialists are patently not infallible, but a measure of respect if the pendulum-swing is not to shake our whole society excessively.

An aspiration shared by nearly all is prosperity, so as prosperity is a common ground objective, then we should be able to approach a number of issues with common criteria from a shared standpoint. Take for example the phenomenon variously known as overmanning, feather bedding, or euphemistically, make-work, but which is far more serious and anti-social in the real meaning of the term, for it is really divorcing work from its social function, labour's rights from labour's duties.

It is absurd and anti-social to claim that men should be kept in work places – whether at the expense of the employer, or more usually, of the taxpayers, the national economy, the British public – going through the motions of working and being paid for it, when their work is actually making no contribution to the national wealth-creating process. It may well be destroying wealth, not creating it, consuming fuel, raw materials, semi-finished goods, many of them imported, as well as credits and a heavy wage bill. This holds good whether the plants are obsolete from economic causes or technical causes, or simply because more workers are kept on than are needed. Overmanning and make-work cannot be justified in the name of socialism of any variety, certainly not in the name of Marxist theory. Marx took as the cornerstone of his economics, as Smith and Ricardo did before him, the labour theory of value, according to which value is created by 'socially necessary labour'.

No socialist economic theories advocate or justify make-work. The Communist countries have no place for it in their theory.

Make-work, the subsidised employment of labour for its own sake divorced from its economic function is neither capitalist nor socialist, but simply opportunist. It stems from appeasement, for the sake of narrow short term party or group political profit, of the most atavistic and anachronistic trade union instincts thinly disguised in socialist rationalisation. We have a lot to do in order to improve the labour market, the fit between people and jobs, labour mobility. These changes have been delayed and sacrificed to make-work and overmanning. Because over-manning increases our costs and makes us less competitive, overmanning creates rather than cures unemployment. Overmanning reduces profits and therefore cuts investment and new employment. Overmanning destroys more jobs than it saves.

Here is an issue on which we and socialists could find common ground. Now you may object that though my critique is justified in theory, it will be rejected by the Labour leaders in practice precisely because they *are* opportunists. But things are not so simple as that. Realities are coming to the aid of realism. Mr. Wilson's government is now in such straits that they cannot afford to hand out subsidies to all and sundry in order to protect overmanning and to rescue jobs, for the very simple reason that the wealth producing base has been eroded to a point where it cannot maintain an ever-expanding wealth-eating superstructure. When the state share of the GNP was a third and the private wealth-producing sector two thirds, the latter managed to keep the former, though the growing weight gradually wore it down, as we now see. Now that the state sector, the wealth consuming sector is nearly twice as large as the residual private wealth producing sector, the socialists are obliged to re-think their whole strategy, like it or not. Some cry forward, some cry back, but they cannot stay as they are.

After all, the Duffy Committee[10] has gone most of the way towards saying this in the context of BLM, much bolder than many of us might have been: the tide is now on the turn, it is up to us to take it at the flood.

If we press, argue, debate this issue, that make-work destroys the economy, makes everyone poorer than they would otherwise be as it spreads like dry rot, we can gain very wide acceptance for our view, so that it will become common ground – understood by the people as essential to prosperity and welcomed by Labour ministers who have come to their wits' end to find cash for their 'wounded heroes' as Mr. Wilson now calls them.

Let me give another example of common understanding in support of common ground objectives, the inflation /unemployment merry-go-round. Barely a year ago, I was subjected to great approbrium by socialist leaders (and not only by socialists) for a speech at Preston in which I argued that the whole pseudo-Keynesian conjuring trick by which inflationary demand creation could apparently maintain perpetual full employment and growth had visibly collapsed in bankruptcy. I also argued that we had misread the unemployment statistics, exaggerated labour availability, under-stating vacancies, creating demand for a stage army of unemployed, and that as a result of these misguided policies, we were creating a real army of unemployed.

I was violently denounced for my speech by Wilson, Benn, Healey and Foot, accused of distortion, of wanting unemployment as a weapon against the workers. A few weeks ago on the speech's anniversary I took the opportunity to quote what Mr. Wilson, Mr. Healey, Mr. Foot had said then, and contrast it with what they are saying and doing now, under pressure of events. Here, too, there is hope for common understanding, because it is now in the interests of the Labour Government and its supporters to recognise realities in this field, to stress the real level of vacancies, to bring home to all concerned that inflationary demand policies will not help but actually make things worse.

There is even hope that we can reach common understanding of the essential need for good profits if we are to secure the common ground objective of prosperity. Many, though not yet enough, of the people understand that job security, good pay, good working conditions and increased investment all depend on adequate profit and that, provided this is earned in competition, the interests of the consumer and of the nation are served.

There are signs that even the government is beginning to move towards this understanding. But it has someway to go yet. Until price control is abolished leaving prices to competition and anti-monopoly legislation, understanding of the need for profit will remain largely platonic.

From what I have said, you will gather that I see the search for common ground as the elaboration of a mental map we can honestly share. This is the exact opposite of opportunistic assent to views or expedients with which we are really out of sympathy but which we think may win votes. We believe that we can now hope to find common ground on overmanning, on investment criteria, on the indispensable role of profit, by whatever name you care to call it and, above all, the need for a rational approach to economic problems. Given such a measure of common ground, one needs no coalition, since the government of the day can rely on responsible opposition. Without such a measure of common ground, coalition will be out of the question anyway.

But of course, the quest for common ground must not be confined to economic policy. Housing, education, social policy have all reached a dead end and where the common assumptions of the middle ground need re-examining in the light of experience and commonsense.

Take housing: can we afford to allow housing policies to continue to fly in the face of economic logic? By simultaneously increasing demand and decreasing supply, we are ineluctably increasing homelessness. Do the socialists want that?

There are equally searching doubts that are so widely shared on social policy, on issues of crime and other issues as well, as to constitute a huge area of potential common ground between politicians and the vast majority of the people. Millions of parents, million of households are waiting for policies that will achieve their purposes – housing choice, decent education, less dependency, less crime.

The vast majority of people of all social strata want a law-abiding society, for when respect for the law weakens, they feel personally insecure. Politically motivated contempt for law and order – or, should I say, emotively-generated contempt for law and order rationalised in left-wing ideology, is confined mainly to a small stratum of intellectuals, semi-intellectuals and hooligans.

Most people in this country regard family life as good. They will judge policies in light of their impact on family life, provided that this is made clear to them. They want to feel that opportunity exists, and that people should feel free to decide whether they should try to struggle to the top of a particular ladder or, indeed, build their own, or give more of their time and energy to other things. People want a safety net, but do not want to see it overloaded. They want no one to fall below a decent level.

To want to provide decent minimum standards is not only different from but opposed to cutting everyone down to the same level, imposing a dreary uniformity that destroys everything that English men and women of all walks of life and occupations consider most worthwhile. We have been misled into forgetting the distinction between maintaining minimum standards and making everything uniform. This distinction has for long been peculiarly clearly understood in England; and we now want to restore it to the centre of our thinking and not let ourselves be confused by muddled talk of 'welfare' and 'equality', which is not the same as providing for 'minimum standards'.

People would like there to be growth, to feel that things get better as time goes on, given the ups and downs of individuals. They will understand that growth has costs, just like everything else, and that they must either accept the social costs of growth, for the sake of its fruits, or make less demands ont the future of growth in order to avoid the costs.

Are large, unstreamed comprehensive schools really ideal structures for education of those who most need to benefit from school – the children from housing estates and older urban areas?

The Labour Party which twenty years ago seemed to be the guardian angel of education has now been systematically subordinating it to political doctrinal objectives and thereby destroying it. The common ground, common ground with the people, in education is that education is about teaching *all* the young as well as possible to read, write and number, to be sufficiently well-informed and self-disciplined to think for themselves and use their minds well, and to be motivated and enabled to earn their living by making the best use of their talents in existing opportunities for productive work. Any discussion of schools that does not start from this purpose and direct everything towards it is not about education, as it is understood by most men and women in England.

A basic difference between democratic and authoritarian government is that in free societies, it is the job of government to find ways of enabling the values, aspirations and purposes of the people to be implemented. In authoritarian societies the government imposes its values and objectives on society.

The socialists have gone a long way recently in imposing their values, which often conflicted with those of a majority of the population of all social strata, in the belief that Socialism's job is to change people, whether they want to change or not, not to serve them.

But most people want to be served, not to be changed. In our pursuit of the middle ground, we grudgingly accepted and tolerated the Socialist desire to impose values on people, rather than ascertain their own and serve them. Fortunately, people have been less easy to change than politicians. So we can still go back to the people, the bedrock of all our policies, and our common ground begins with them.

Freedom, freedom within the law to run our own lives, is a value. So far it is not everybody's objective. It is our task as politicians and opinion formers to ensure that it becomes and remains an objective. For people do not automatically support freedom in the abstract; they aspire to concrete freedom to achieve certain goals and avoid certain constraints. They have to be persuaded anew in each generation that their particular freedom is best guaranteed by freedom within the law for all; even though freedom for others can constitute a limitation on their own freedom, the absence of freedom for others can threaten the continued existence of their own.

But by and large, we can argue for a presupposition in favour of freedom on the part of most people. It is an issue which divides socialists, and not necessarily along any left-right cleavage. It is up to us to oblige those among them that share our concern for freedom, shared by most people, to face up to the implications of many of their policies. It is up to us to show that many socialist measures, even though they may have been undertaken in the belief that they would extend freedom, are effectually curtailing or undermining it.

Freedom and order are, I believe, complementary not antagonistic. Most people also have a natural instinct for order and rationality. They are appalled by waste, inefficiency, obvious irrationality. It is this instinct which was utilised by advocates of socialism, who have traditionally presented the apparent chaos of the market economy, exaggerating its worst features, ignoring its best achievements which remain at the apex of human endeavour, and contrasted it with idealised socialism. Perhaps we were bound to lose ground when we had to oppose the socialist shining utopian ideal with arguments based on our shopsoiled reality, particularly as it was made progressively worse by well-meaning intervention. By now, however, after 30 years of the new dispensation, people are prepared to recognise that we have no longer a broadly self-regulating system, but a more and more socialist system, with induced chaos, and criticise it for what it is.

On subsequent occasions, I shall try to trace the basis for common ground in various fields of policy in greater detail.

Suffice to say here that the present crisis gives us more than an opportunity to change our mood, methods and policies, it obliges us to re-think our position, just as it does the socialists. For whatever else may unite or divide us, one thing at least is agreed: things cannot go on as they are.

And for every socialist or socialist supporter who cries 'forward . . . more of the same', there must be many who must stop to ask themselves what has gone wrong? How did the proud confident morning of 1945 lead to the twilight of 1975? And we Conservatives full share this need to question. After all, we have held power for half of the past 30 years; how did we allow things to come to such a pass? We must ask the questions not from any mood of self-inculpation, but because a proper understanding of where we went astray is essential to finding the way forward.

The majority of the people of this country share our realization that the country has gone astray, our resolve to find the way forward and our confidence that it can be done. This is the bedrock of the common ground we seek. However far we are able to extend this common ground in months and years to come, there will still remain much at issue between the parties and inside the parties. But our debate could become so better informed, so more fruitful if it began from the quest for maximum common ground, as this country has enjoyed in the past, when it was one ingredient of greatness, and if we will it, can become so again.

Oxford Union
6 December 1975

NOTES

1. *Criminal Statistics* 1975, Cmnd. 6566, HMSO 1976.
2. *National Income and Expenditure,* 1965-1975, *Blue Book,* HMSO 1976.
3. 'And if you still despair', *Economist,* 3 January 1976.
   James Pool 'Go West (if you can) young man', *Sunday Times* 11 January 1976.
4. Harold Macmillan, *The Middle Way* (Macmillan, 1938).
5. J. C. R. Dow, chpt II, 'The Labour Chancellors, 1945-1951; *The Management of the British Economy* 1945-1960 (Cambridge University Press 1968).
6. *General Theory of Employment, Interest and Money,* John Keynes (Macmillan 1936).
7. Housing Act, 1974, HMSO.
8. Stuart Holland's, *The Socialist Challenge* (Quartet Books, 1975); *Strateg y for Socialism: The Challenge of Labour's Programme* (Bertrand Russell Peace Foundation for Spokesman Books, 1975); *Capital versus the Regions* (Macmillan, 1976); *The Regional Problem* (Macmillan, 1976).
9. Samuel Brittan, *Left or Right The Bogus Dilemma* (Secker and Warburg, 1968).
10. *The Motor Vehicles Industry,* HC 617, HMSO 1975.

GOVERNMENT SPENDING GENERATES UNEMPLOYMENT

CONTROVERSY surrounding Mr. Healey's White Paper[1] on government expenditure is now gaining its second wind. As we have already made clear, and shall continue to make clear, the Government's strategy is fundamentally wrong. Instead of cutting government expenditure, they plan to increase it, though Mr. Healey says that it will increase by less than it might otherwise have done, a new addition to new-speak.

Moreover, the real implications are distorted by over-optimistic estimates of the rate of growth.

We shall argue against Mr. Healey's spending policies in general and in detail. On this occasion I wish to confine myself to one aspect of the argument, the oft-repeated excuse by Mr. Healey and his colleagues, that even if Government is over-spending, it helps make work, and that if overspending were halted, additional unemployment would be caused.

I shall argue that this is the exact opposite of the truth. That, in fact, Government overspending is a major and continued cause of unemployment. I shall reaffirm my conviction that cuts in runaway state expenditure are essential if we are to save the economy and eventually restore a high and stable level of employment.

Of course, at first sight, the socialists' contention does seem quite plausible, doesn't it? Government spending keep people employed; if you cut it, then they will cease to be employed. But when you look at the overall picture you see the catch. Let me explain.

In a sense, the socialists' contention that government spending keeps up employment is a variant of their former, now discredited, argument that a high level of monetary demand will keep up employment and this justifies eapanding the money supply.

Do you remember the storm of abuse directed at me and some of my colleagues when we argued, only eighteen months ago, that use of the 'printing press' was no way to create full employment and growth, that in all but the very short run it could only result in stagnation and growing unemployment?[2]

When we said that the time had come to stop the printing presses, we were accused of wanting unemployment, as though someone who warns you to take your umbrella wants rain.

Then, as you know, we stuck to our guns, refused to be overawed by abuse and imputations and argued back. Within a year of the October 1974 election which the socialists fought on the promise of full employment, by fiat, by act of will and use of the printing press, Mr. Wilson, Mr. Healey, Mr. Foot *et al* reversed their stand. They admitted that contrary to what they had been telling us inflation does not save jobs but, on the contrary, destroys them.[3]

A sinner come to judgement brings more joy to heaven than 99 righteous men. But unfortunately, as we see, the Labour Party's renunciation of the sin of inflationeering has gone only half way at best. Because they now take refuge in a variant of their 1974 election refrain. They now say that government spending maintains employment, not full employment, but fuller. That government over-spending is good so long as it is not financed by the printing press, but is raised by taxation, borrowing from the public and borrowing abroad. I contest this and argue that government over-spending has depressed the level of employment below what it would otherwise have been.

Now borrowing from abroad has only one drawback; you have to pay it back, with interest.[4] Unless it is used to increase the country's capacity to produce and export, foreign borrowing is simply a deferred balance of payments crisis.

In this context, it is worth noting that Labour's claim that they can afford to borrow now and pay back out of princely North Sea oil revenues which we questioned at the time, is now admitted by them to be so much window dressing. They have admitted this in the context of the Labour split in Scotland, warning the Scots not to place too much faith in the value of North Sea oil, since it is high cost and very vulnerable. What a pity that the Socialists have one story to tell the Scots and another to tell south of the border, just as they have one for us, one for their paymasters in the IMF.

But apart from foreign borrowing, which is piling up problems for years to come and which is already pressed to its limits, finance for government expenditure can come from three sources: printing, borrowing from the public and taxation. Since the socialists now agree that 'printing money' creates more problems than it solves they are left with taxation and borrowing from the public to finance their public expenditure.

But both these expedients, excessive taxation and excessive borrowing are important components in the sluggishness of the private sector, for the downturn in production and employment.

The burden of taxation, punitive and inflation-blind taxation, together with price controls and other impositions on the business sector, has been crippling, compounded by the recession brought on in part by these ill-conceived measures. The overall rate of profit is now a fraction of what it was. Together with the wage increases forced on employers by this Government, by Mr. Foot and Mr. Healey, irrespective of each industry's economic position each firm's ability to pay, these pressures have led to bankruptcies, short-time, redundancies. They could not possibly have done otherwise.

State borrowing from the public, by government and local authorities, competes for limited funds with borrowing by private firms. The state, central and local, is in a strong position. It is a safe borrower, or at least has been so far, and it can push up its interest rates knowing that the public will have to pay the extra in form of taxes or rates. The plethora of local authority Olympic swimming pools, new town halls, council flats with enormous subsidies, leisure centres, civic centres, as well as heavy investment in nationalized industries which is rendered nugatory by their manpower policies, all these are at the expense of private industry and, hence, of employment.

So, with price controls, taxes, wage demands and low or even negative rates of profit, the private sector cannot take as much labour as it otherwise might. And let me add, Denis Healey's attempt to cure the symptoms of this by his so-called employment protection[5] measures will not protect employment in any but the shortest of short runs. Michael Foot's compulsory employment measures[6] will do the opposite. They will force more firms into bankruptcy which would otherwise have got by. They will deter firms from taking on more workers, if they are to be like the old man of the sea: once on their back they will never got off.

We know the rest of the story. Unemployment, however you measure it, has reached its highest level since the War.[7]

This has forced all of us to look afresh at the recent economic history of the United Kingdom, and in particular at the so-called Keynesian full employment economics, which has as little to do with Keynes as with full employment, that dominated our thinking and policy since the Second World War.

One of the mechanistic assumptions of the pseudo-Keynesians has been that the level of aggregate demand automatically and ineluctably determines the level of employment and, hence, of unemployment. But this is misleading. The level of aggregate demand is only one of many factors which affects the levels of employment and unemployment, as Keynes himself always made quite clear.

Another factor which affects unemployment levels is mobility of labour, between jobs that is to say, though this can, of course, sometimes entail geographical mobility, willingness to travel further to work or, even, in some cases to move. It can entail occupational mobility, that is to say willingness to take what job is going, rather than waiting for the same kind of job.

When mobility of labour is low, we can have more unemployed co-existing with more unfilled vacancies at a given level of aggregate demand, than you would have with that same level of demand were the mobility of labour greater.

Another strong influence on the volume of unemployment is the matter of wage levels in relation to output, the way in which groups of workers can price themselves out of jobs sometimes under the misapprehension that the Government could and should somehow immunise them from the effects of their own acts.

A further factor is the level of entrepreneurship and management, the existence of people who can both identify demand, mobilise the resources and satisfy it for a profit, which is partly determined by society's attitude to them, not least tax policies.

In each respect our performance, mobility, wage levels, treatment of wealth-creators, operates against jobs rather than in favour of them.

The deployment of complementary resources is another factor determining employment levels given aggregate demand. Every industry and firm has a different level of capital needed to employ a quantum of workers. If some firms, nationalized or subsidized, are given resources by the State to permit them to produce goods and services at above economic cost, to continue with technologically obsolete labour-intensive methods, or to overman, this can only be at the expense of the level of turnover and, hence, employment which would otherwise be achieved in other firms and branches. At best, this would be putting Peter on the dole to keep Paul in work. But insofar as the 'job-protection' subsidies are given to firms and industries with a high complementary resources ratio, i.e. which need above average quanta of working and fixed capital per worker employed, then they will destroy more jobs than they save.

Several Peters go on the dole for every Paul kept in a protected job. Several wealth-creating private sector Peters are thrown out of work. The saved jobs are identifiable and concentrated: the lost jobs are anonymous and dispersed.

Now you will find that this is precisely the pattern of 'job-protection'. As you know, between three and four hundred-thousand people join the unemployment register every month from choice or necessity and roughly the same number find jobs and leave the register, sometimes more, sometimes less. This is a normal part of the life of any economy, the greater the dynamism, the faster the flow, particularly in times of readjustment. No government could conceivably lash out subsidies to stop the three-hundred-thousand a month or any sizeable proportion losing their current work. The cost would be out of the question. Moreover, if people do not leave jobs, there is a shortage of people to fill the new jobs needed for growth. So on what principle does the government decide to step in with large sums to 'preserve' certain jobs, a fraction of the total which are really falling redundant in any month? The considerations are not economic. Nor are they 'social', a term socialists love to use without definition, criteria, or measurement, to throw a cloak of respectability over motives of narrow party expediency. How can it be 'social' to lavish hundreds of millions of pounds worth of resources in keeping men going through the motions of work bereft of social value, when both the complementary resources and labour might be better employed. And how can it be social to make the taxpayer, which includes the low-paid, subsidise highly paid car workers to perform uneconomic activities, particularly when their enterprises' unviability stems at least in part from their own actions. No, the basis for 'job preservation' is wholly political, often crudely partly political, often under pressure from a politically powerful union.[8]

Now where are these firms or industries with politically powerful union groupings to squeeze public money out of the government to maintain economically unjustified jobs? They tend to be where large concentrations of union labour exist, particularly the nationalized industries.

In many such cases there are high concentrations of capital, working and fixed, per worker. The employments where unions have strong enough political muscle to blackmail governments into subsidies to maintain economically unnecessary jobs are generally those which need substantial sums of working capital per worker kept on. Hence the high cost of job protection.

Take British Rail.[9] How much does each job saved there cost us? Let us add up. First, there is an operating deficit of some four hundred million. Then there is a capital deficit, estimated at some two thousand million pounds of public money in grants and write-offs. The word 'write-off' is misleading, because the debt remains and the British taxpayer has to redeem it.

Or, if you care to look at it in terms of resources, thousands of millions of pounds worth of resources have been poured into the railways. They give us a negative return at present but could be productively used, either by making the railways pay or, by putting them to other uses, for example turning uneconomic railways and their stations into express bus routes and terminals.

So, in addition to the four hundred million operating deficit, we are fully justified in adding debt servicing on the two billion. I think that ten per cent per annum is a very low figure. So, this makes a total of six hundred million a year in subsidy. Now the main purpose of this subsidy is to keep more rail union members in work than would otherwise be used. The annual cost for jobs saved is prodigious: well into five figures per job per year. Take the cost per job saved at British Leyland and Chrysler. And bear in mind too, that the Ryder Report[10] under-estimated the likely costs and over-estimated possible revenues, as the all-party Select Committee pointed out. The cost is not the cost of keeping all BLM and Chrysler workers in jobs, or even those budgeted for. It is the difference between those who would have remained in work in the British motor-car industry, if the enterprises had been slimmed down, and those who will be working over the next few years. The figure per job saved per year comes out very high.

These resources are used uneconomically, just as labour is used uneconomically, for the sake of activity, not for the sake of creating wealth. Production, not to satisfy need, but for appearance sake. And the price can be counted in money, living standards, and, irony of ironies, in jobs.

As we see, though Mr. Wilson and his colleagues will talk about picking the winners, the actual system makes sure that they finance the losers.[11] For the pressures from trade unions with members in overmanned declining industries and firms will always be greater than the pressures from unions in industries which should be growing, in turnover or manpower.

Hence British socialism leads inexorably to inefficiency and stagnation in spite of all fine words about planning. That is why we say that Labour is the party of unemployment. By throwing good money after bad in propping up inefficient enterprises, at very high cost, they are creating even more unemployment week by week.

So what is to be done? Public spending should be cut; the savings should be used partly to reduce borrowing and partly to reduce taxes, particularly in ways likely to increase the confidence and the profits of the business sector on which the whole economy depends.

But, Mr. Wilson and Mr. Healey will argue that they cannot cut Government expenditure before the private sector takes up the slack or more jobs will fall, that there will be a gap of time between cutting state spending and revived private spending. So there will. But let all concerned realise that if they do not cut state spending now, soon, many more private sector jobs will be lost in the near future to pay for the maintained indeed, the increased, state spending.

The questions are not, therefore, 'what will you cut?' and 'how much unemployment would you cause?'. The unemployment is bound to rise either way, in the state sector or the private sector.

Either way, their way or our way, there will be some increased unemployment. Their way is a cul-de-sac, a continuingly bloated wealth-consuming state sector and a dwindling more and more debilitated wealth-creating private sector, with fewer and fewer jobs. Our way is the road to recovery, fewer jobs in the state sector, but less loss of jobs in the private sector and, after an interval, more jobs, self-sustaining, wealth-creating, tax-base jobs in the private sector.

The Government is wrong, therefore, to argue that it must keep up state spending to avoid extra unemployment. State spending will, itself, cause extra unemployment in the private sector. Let the transfer, the health restoring transfer from the state to the private sector, begin soon.

Harrow
6 March 1976

NOTES

1. *Public Expenditure* to 1979/80, Cmnd. 6393, HMSO, 1976; *Hansard,* Cols. 2010-2033, 22 July, 1976, HMSO, 1976.
2. *The Times,* 7 September 1974.
3. *Attack on Inflation,* Cmnd. 6151, HMSO 1975.
4. Estimates of PSBR for 1976-77 and 1977-78 is £11·5 billion and £9 billion respectively.
5. Temporary Employment Subsidy, Budget Statement, April 1976, *Hansard,* HMSO.
6. *Employment Protection Act,* 1975, HMSO 1975.
7. Mid-August, 1976 figure of 1·5 million. Accounts for 6·4 per cent of the labour force.
8. 'Towards the Parasite State', Paul Johnson, *New Statesman,* 3 September 1976.
9. Sir Richard Marsh, Chairman's retirement interview, *Daily Telegraph,* 10 September 1976.
10. H. C. 342, HMSO, 1975.
11. B. Hindley, *Industrial Merger and Public Policy* (Institute of Economic Affairs, 1970).

ECONOMIC CONSEQUENCES OF THE SOCIAL CONTRACT

THE pound is falling day by day.[1] What do our socialist masters in government and trades unions do about it? Some of them blame foreign banks, while they rush cap in hand to them for help. But can anything help until government and unions understand why the pound is falling, as a preliminary to stopping the fall?

The value of a currency is a reflection of the strength and rationality of the country's economy. Where people are allowed to get on with their productive work, where government and unions are co-operative towards change, you will have a strong economy, and hence a strong currency. Conversely, where government ravage the country's resources, human and material, for short-term political convenience, ideological fads and vendettas, and where unions obstruct economic progress while demanding its fruits in advance, you will have a weak economy and, hence, a weak currency.

It is feckless government spending which is the main cause in the fall in the value of the pound sterling.[2]

We now have a weak economy, the weakest in our history and, hence, the weakest pound.

There are no secrets in economics. Everyone knows what is happening here. Foreign banks have offices in the City. Foreign embassies have economics departments, they read the official statistics no less than the speeches and debates and specialist writings. So they sell sterling and down goes the pound even further.

Why has the government over-spent by several billion pounds over the last few years?[3] They knew better, but they preferred to curry favour with union leaders and their own left-wing by nationalizing, by subsidizing, by encouraging demand, by discouraging supply, by vindictive taxation and endless regulation.

They have increased the load on the productive sector and the economy to a point where it staggers under the burden of taxation, legislation and price-control imposed to buy union and left-wing approval.

But the more money government spends, the more it has to tax or borrow or print, and this is what the foreign observer watches, seeing only too clearly that unless government cuts public spending we shall get worse inflation and worse unemployment.

In other words, the more the government tries to pander to union and left-wing prejudices, the worse things will get and, the worse things get, the more strained government relations with the trades union leaders become. These are the economic consequences of the social contract.

To halt the slide the government must reverse its policies and cut government spending to levels we can afford, cutting subsidies to housing, food, make-work, lame ducks.

There is no other way.

True, the unions will not like it.[4] But neither will the unions like the results of the present rake's progress, with employment falling as the economy slows down under the burden, with more foreign loans and eventually, after we are even deeper in debt, harsher terms attached, and with every likelihood of rising inflation and rising unemployment as the government is forced to print money if it will not cut its own spending.

Either way, the union leaders will not like what happens. This government is in for difficulties whether it does right or wrong. But if it does wrong and goes on overspending, its difficulties are bound to become worse. So let the government give up its rake's progress of the past two and a quarter years and put the country's interests first, follow principle instead of convenience, logic instead of magic.

Sarrat
Hertfordshire
3 June 1976

NOTES

1. Since 1971 the £ has depreciated by 40 per cent.
2. Bank of England Quarterly Bulletin, September 1976; Samuel Brittan, 'How we manufacture our sterling orises', *Financial Times,* 16 September 1976.
3. During 1974-1975 the PSBR exceeded its budget estimate by £3,000 million.
4. TUC conference debate 8 September 1976. Congress promises to give full support to members fighting cuts in public expenditure.

RECOVERY WITHOUT INFLATION

IRVING FRIEDMAN[1] covered a wide field; I must confine my response to two principal theses. The first relates to the ambiguity of the theme 'Recovery without Inflation', which seems to imply a choice between recovering with or without inflation. I shall argue that the real choice is between recovery without inflation and no recovery at all.

My second thesis is that the eradication of inflation entails solving the problems created by unbridled political intervention in economic life, mainly by governments. For such intervention tends to encourage demand while discouraging supply, generating the scarcity to which Irving Friedman referred. We are now suffering as much from remedies imposed since the Second World War as from the ills they were designed to cure.

This is not an argument about state versus private ownership but about the disruptive impact on economic progress and social cohesion of the overweening political power of our time. What I shall be saying is that governments have limited powers for good, though unlimited for ill, and that these powers depend on understanding the social and economic process and working with it to achieve the best of alternative outcomes.

You would prefer me to speak from what I know best. I draw my ideas mainly from British experience but am aware that with the change of names, and percentages, the story can be told of us all – or nearly all. I am not an economist but a politician who has had to learn his economics as best he could, from practice to theory.

What you expect from me is not primarily economic analysis, which you could do at least as well as I, but the economics of politics and the politics of economics.[2]

And politics is not just about institutions but about ideas, which form the climate within which decisions are taken.

Irving Friedman correctly points out that though inflation is nothing new, the present wave of world inflation is qualitatively new in scope, duration and apparent intractability, and in its association with domestic and world recession.[3] I shall add that its novelty stems from its political character; it is politically-induced inflation, caused by governments, not least by those who talk most about fighting it.

You may object that political inflation is nothing new. Kings and Emperors went in for currency debasement almost as soon as there was currency to debase. But there was a difference. Debasement of the coinage was recognised to be morally wrong and eventually self-defeating, even by those who committed it.

The issue of paper money not backed by gold was regarded as a temporary expedient justifiable only in exceptional circumstances.

Until quite recently money seemed to be something objective, wholly or largely independent of government and institutions. In our own lifetime the situation has changed dramatically. Money is now something created by governments at will. Its creation, no less than its use once created, is seen as an instrument of economic policy. This politicization of money-creation is now widely accepted as legitimate indeed, indispensable.

This is part of a wider transformation of attitudes towards economic policy in general. Until a couple of generations ago not only money but economic life itself were seen as largely objective, independent of the will of government, though not immune from influence by it. The concept of the government-made or government-controlled economy was relegated to the fringes of modern society: on the one side to diehards in the authoritarian pre-capitalist regimes, Czarist Russia, Imperial Germany, Spain, and on the other to nascent Socialist movements. Paradoxically, during the heyday of the market economy in Europe, it was the right which favoured economic controls while the left of centre favoured the widest economic freedoms, regarding all state regulation as self-defeating. By now, protagonists have turned half a circle. Simultaneously, the focus of debate has moved from the desirability and feasibility of state control of economic life to the means and ends.

We must ask ourselves why this intellectual transformation occurred and why it has maintained, even strengthened, its hold over educated opinion, in spite of the set-backs, calamities and disappointments which the application of these ideas has occasioned as Irving Friedman has demonstrated so cogently.[4] How did we reach this state of affairs after several centuries of economic growth paralleled by increasing acceptance of the principles of the free economy in a free society on which the seal seemed to have been set exactly two centuries back, with Adam Smith's widely acclaimed *Wealth of Nations*?[5]

How do we explain what seems to many of us an intellectual regression?

Unless we can explain it, I should be less than optimistic regarding our ability to do much about it.

The mood of interventionism in general and in particular the category with which we have become familiar in the West during our own lifetime has its origin in several sources.

For a start, we should neither ignore nor disparage the inherent human desire for greater control over our own economic and social destiny which provided much of the moral dynamic for the trends under discussion. I criticize the interventionists not so much for what they aspired to do, but precisely because they have proven largely counter-productive in their own terms, leaving us with less control, not more, rousing economic tempests rather than quieting them. But it remains true that unless we can offer sound feasible paths to whatever measure of control over our economic environment is feasible, through greater understanding in the first place, the quacks and utopians will rush in to fill the vacuum.

Secondly, the expansion of the non-business sector of society has brought with it the greater urge to interference. Expanded social studies departments, new professors, new research, new government departments all tend to generate pressures for more central power at the expense of the business sector. This trend all too easily becomes self-perpetuating since every failure occasioned by the new burdens and distortions is adduced as the need for further intervention, to a point where the burdens created weaken the whole basis on which they rest.

But reflection has convinced me that none of these developments can be explained without reference to the impact of two world wars. War, which includes preparations for war and its aftermath, has always played an important part in shaping society and economic life. The two world wars impelled society towards interventionism and socialism in a number of ways.

First, war, the militarization of society, entails confiding vast additional powers to government, legitimizes these powers in the name of patriotism, indeed of national survival. Once granted, they or the vested interests which they generate, tend to perpetuate themselves.

Secondly, war evokes the promise of a better future for all classes once war ends, a land fit for heroes, while simultaneously weakening the economy and burdening it with huge debts. So at war's end the demand for prosperity is intensified by the economic optical illusion created by war; government mobilization of human and material resources to win the war suggests that it should be possible to do the same to win the peace. We know the answers but they have been muted.

In Britain, after the human and economic blood-letting of the First World War, we tried to go back overnight to pre-war normality as seen through rose-tinted spectacles, ignoring the economic disruption caused by war and the long overdue restructuring that the economy needed in any case.

The self-deception was symbolized by the decision in 1925 to restore the pound sterling to its pre-war gold parity, to 'look the dollar in the face' in spite of all that had transpired since 1914, repeating the mistake made a century earlier against Ricardo's warnings. This ensured that the depression would reach England sooner, last longer, go deeper and undermine belief in the self-regenerative powers of the economy. It also created the climate in which short-term remedies sought by and under Conservatives paved the way for socialist measures and what came to be known as Keynesian full-employment and growth policies. This is actually a misnomer: not only were many of the ideas foreign to Keynes, but they have brought the very opposite of full employment and sustained growth.

Keynesism was a symptom of the mood rather than its cause. Many ideas were fathered onto Keynes which had not been his and which ran counter to his inclinations.[6] But the mood created a climate within which critics were quiet, partly for fear of being said to want unemployment and other ills which the neo-Keynesians and socialists claimed to be able to cure by their panaceas. In part too, Keynesism was grasped as an alternative to full-blooded Socialism whereas, in practise, it has paved the way for socialist advance.

At all events, the prestige of Keynes's name was used to add respectability to the pursuit of a high sustained level of employment, soon to be translated into an excess of demand for labour over supply, and high growth rates by the simple expedient of expansionary demand measures by government.

It was argued by pseudo-Keynesians that to keep the money supply growth to the levels needed to avoid inflation would, given the imperfection of the labour market and structural obsolescence in the economy, impose stagnation and mass unemployment. This always was a misleading half-truth, for three good reasons. First, as we have seen, with an imperfect labour market made even more imperfect as a result of government measures, and structural obsolescence shored up by government aid, there could be no hope of escaping relative stagnation and either high under-employment or mass unemployment. Inflationary demand expansion not only cannot ward them off but, indeed, after temporary relief, ensures that they will be worse than they otherwise would have been while at the same time producing an excuse for putting off the real cures.

Secondly, the level of demand is only one of the factors which go to determine growth, employment, well-being, as Keynes well knew but his followers forgot. Other factors include the efficiency of the labour market and of capital markets, the rewards to work, enterprise, innovation and efficiency, the level of saving, the willingness of labour and government to co-operate with change in deeds as well as words.

Thirdly, in an economy like Britain's with a high foreign-trade quotient, there is always great need and endless room for expansion into world markets, whereas expansion of domestic demand by deficit financing can only upset the balance of payments and set off a downwards spiral. But the Keynesian short cut to Utopia won the political auction.

We are now living with the results.[7] This high-demand strategy, imposed on a complex economy intricately involved with the world economic system, soon began to prove counter-productive.

In Britain, the level of demand needed to bring down the number of registered unemployed in the older industrial areas to levels considered 'politically acceptable' caused inflation, unsettled the whole economy, sucking in large numbers of unskilled labourers from abroad and straining the balance of payments.

Attempts to remedy this by cutting demand predictably created withdrawal symptoms including increased unemployment which in turn, led to pressures for reflation. The apparent dilemma between inflation and balance of payment difficulties on the one hand, and unemployment and stagnation on the other, should have led policy makers to question their high-demand strategy. Instead, partisans of the new, *soi disant* Keynesian methods argued that it needed control over wages and prices to make it work.

Intellectually, they ignored a basic tenet of economics that the quantity of money, like the quantity of anything else, influences its price, that is its value. They failed to produce a definition of inflation, which I should define as a sustained upward pressure on the general price level generated by an excess of monetary demand over the supply of goods and services. Instead, they equated inflation with any price increases, and supposed that price increases were simply caused by other price increases and, therefore, that if some price increases were suppressed no others would follow.

This attempt to suppress the effects or symptoms of inflation by controlling prices and wages has been accompanied in Britain by maintained or even increased public spending and by other policies and measures sought by the union leaders as the price of their co-operation. The combined result has predictably been more inflationary than deflationary.[8]

The additional expenditures have been financed partly by creating new money, partly by foreign borrowing, partly by borrowing from the public at the expense of the private sector, partly by additional taxation levied on the private sector.

Holding down prices increases consumption and effectively expands consumer purchasing power while impinging on the private sector's profitability.

This decline in profitability was masked at first by inflation, even going unrecognised by firms themselves, given conservatism on the part of sectors of the accounting profession. In many cases, firms which have actually moved into a deficitary position go on showing healthy nominal profits on which they are taxed and obliged to pay dividends. Their lack of profitability appears, in the first place, as a cash-flow problem, credit shortage. But the recent decline by over half in post-tax profits as a share in GNP was bound to depress investment, and to intensify the combined effects of price control and increased wage and other costs on turnover and, hence, on employment.[9] I am not discussing last month's trade figures but the progression of the past thirty years.

So a vicious circle of decline and inflation is set up. Faced by falling output and employment in the private sector, government is tempted to intensify its expansionary policies, pumping yet more demand into the economy and subsidizing employment in uncompetitive enterprise or branches.

But this additional burden in turn, whether financed by taxing, borrowing or printing, only depresses activity and employment in the private sector still further. Indeed, the kind of 'job protection' undertaken tends to be costly, since it is generally in branches where deficits of several thousands of pounds per worker per year are generated by job protection. As a result, this kind of identifiable and concentrated job-saving, in public or private sector, is matched by a multiple of unidentified jobs destroyed throughout the private sector.

Governments worried by low levels of investment characteristically seek to tackle symptoms rather than causes. Pressures are exerted on banks and financial institutions, including pension funds and insurance companies, to lend to industry without thought as to the reasons why industrial investment has slowed down.

I need not explain to an audience of bankers why enterprises which are unable to generate sufficient retained profits to finance expansion are seldom well advised to expand on borrowed capital. Given the political circumstances, these loans are channelled largely into failing enterprises, often over-manned with a history of bad labour relations. The money is soon swallowed up, leaving the position of the enterprises even worse than before.

At a late stage in inflationary recession even firms with retained profits may deem it wise not to invest them, but may prefer to lend them to government in order to safeguard their own liquidity. So, government borrowing and expenditure on current consumption and unproductive investment grows, while productive investment lags, adding another dimension to the Keynesian nightmare. This might well be called the general crisis of Keynesism.

It follows from this that so long as inflation and, worse still, the measures often used to combat inflation, last there can be no recovery. Industry cannot plan ahead when the level *of costs depends on government caprice,* when its prices are set by politicians and bureaucrats according to short-term political considerations, when government, central and local, will outbid it for credits, professional staff and labour, and then, adding insult to injury, will blame industry for not investing!

In the circumstances the private sector's reaction is to pull in its horns and try to survive till sanity returns.

We entered the age of Keynes believing that inflation was a lesser evil, that a little inflation might even do good. We end with the realization that inflation corrodes and erodes economic activity, making economic life nasty, brutish and above all short-term, eroding a base we once took for granted. Far from being a lesser evil, it is a certain source of all conceivable economic, social and political evils.[10]

This is the situation faced today by many Western countries to a greater or lesser degree whether or not they call themselves Keynesians. True, Britain went further than most countries, given our anti-enterprise bias and the less than fully realistic attitude of the unions.[11] But, perhaps for that reason, we may be next in line to liberate outselves. What governments cause, governments can remedy.

If successive governments have brought people to believe that money grows on trees, that it is government's duty and within government's abilities to keep them in jobs however they behave, whatever the nature of the jobs, its social necessity, its cost, then government has no right to blame the workers' intransigence rather than its own lack of resolution.

It should not be beyond our powers to bring this to people's understanding. I believe that people are capable of understanding the truth when it is properly explained to them. With this degree of understanding, I am sure that our public will face and overcome the withdrawal symptoms to be expected when we attempt to abate inflation as a precondition for commencing recovery and a new state of progress.

I leave the last word with Adam Smith.

Two centuries of history have convinced me how right he was.

> The uniform, constant and uninterrupted effort of every man to better his condition, the principle from which public and national, as well as private opulence is originally derived, is frequently powerful enough to maintain the natural progess of things towards improvement, in spite of both the extravagance of government and the greatest errors of administration. Like the unknown principle of animal life, it frequently restores health and vigour to the constitution, in spite not only of the disease, but of the absurd prescriptions of the doctor.

International Monetary Conference
San Francisco
17 June 1976

NOTES

1. Economic Advisor to City Bank.
2. *The Vote Motive,* Gordon Tullock, (Institute of Economic Affairs, 1976).
3. *Inflation: a worldwide disaster,*
4. *ibid.,*
5. Clarendon Press 1976.
6. W. H. Hutt, *Keynesianism – Retrospect and Prospect* (Regenery, 1963); Sir Roy Harrod, *The Life of John Maynard Keynes* (Macmillan, 1951).
7. F. A. Hayek, *Full Employment at any Price* (Institute of Economic Affairs, 1975).
8. John Flemming, *Inflation* (Oxford University Press, 1976).
9. 'Trends in company profitability', *Bank of England Quarterly Bulletin,* March 1976; Andrew Glynn and Bob Sutcliffe, *British Capitalism, Workers and the Profit Squeeze,* (Penguin 1972).
10. F. A. Hayek, *A Tiger by the Tail* (Institute of Economic Affairs, 1972).
11. Paul Johnson, 'Towards the Parasite State', *New Statesman,* 3 September 1976.

MORAL AND MATERIAL BENEFITS OF THE MARKET ORDER

You will all remember the recent shortage of sugar[1]. There is, of course, an international agreement between governments to ensure a steady supply of sugar at a reasonable price to the consumer.[2]

For many years now there have been hospital queues of varying lengths for operations which, though not urgent, could relieve much pain and discomfort.[3] Successive UK governments have, of course, been striving throughout this period to provide prompt, comprehensive and efficient medical care for all.

During the last two years surplus food production in the European Community has created spectacular butter mountains and extensive wine lakes. Of course, European governments have been co-operating in a bold, imaginative scheme of a managed agricultural market in order to avoid the waste and inefficiency of free competition.

There are as yet no shortages of childrens' clothes, colour TVs, or household goods. Nor are there unsaleable surpluses of vacuum cleaners, toys, or ball-point pens. Could this be because government has significantly failed to regulate the production and sale of these goods in the best interest of the community?

You will have gathered by now that I have embarked upon a theme close to my heart. Namely, that the blind, unplanned, unco-ordinated wisdom of the market is overwhelmingly superior to the well-researched, rational, systematic, well-meaning, co-operative, science-based, forward-looking, statistically respectable plans of governments, bureaucracies and international organisations preserved from human error and made thoroughly respectable by the employment of numerous computers.

But this view of mine has been subject to a very considerable criticism. It is argued that the free competitive market does not exist, that it was killed off some years ago and that we, in the Tory Party, are in favour of a ghost.

Let me introduce you to the most confident of the sceptics, Professor J. K. Galbraith, author of the *New Industrial State* and a Past President of the American Economics Society.

According to him the 'modern corporation is no longer subordinate to the market'. Indeed, he argues, that the market is subordinate to the modern corporation:

> The initiative in deciding what is to be produced comes not from the sovereign consumer who, through the market issues the instructions that bend the productive mechanism to his ultimate will. Rather it comes from the great producing organisation which reaches forward to control the markets that it is presumed to serve and, beyond, to bend the customer to its needs. (*The New Industrial State,* p. 6).

And this control is apparently eternal because, according to Professor Galbraith, the organized part of the economy 'protects its profits by planning'.

Professor Galbraith would have us believe that in mocking the conventional pieties he is a courageous iconoclast. In fact it is Professor Galbraith who presents what for twenty years has been the conventional wisdom. Such opinions have dominated the British economic faculties, the financial pages of newspapers, the speeches of our politicians as well as the thinking of our civil servants.

What has been their legacy? As the Romans said: Circumspice!

For the fact is that large corporations and multi-nationals are not immune to the discipline and sanctions of the market. If they were we would not have the all-too recent examples of industrial giants collapsing or going cap in hands to governments for cash aid. Was Rolls-Royce immune? Was Lockheed? Was BSA? Did the once enormous cinema industry plan its own contraction?

And the explanation for this is that there is real competition. Big firms do sometimes collapse and small firms, by satisfying a public demand, grow big. Morphy Richards began by making electric fires in a small barn in 1936.

Fortes was found in 1935 with the opening of a single small shop.[4] In case there are any social scientists present who prefer statistical to anecdotal evidence let me point out that of the largest 100 corporations in the U.S. in 1909, only thirty-six were on the list forty years later.

But what of Galbraith's claim that the consumer is merely clay in the hands of the producer[5] who can bend him to his will through modern techniques of advertising, sales promotion and public relations? Indeed, according to Galbraith, the producer is bound to behave in this way because the degree of advanced commitment which contemporary technological processes involve make it far too risky to rely on the 'untutored responses of the consumer'. The producer therefore sets out to fabricate demand for his goods.

What Professor Galbraith omits to explain is[6] why, if the consumer is as malleable as he suggests, products launched by major firms and accompanied by lavish programmes of advertising and sales promotion frequently fail to find a market. The Ford Edsel car is a spectacular example of the expensive failure which, if the Galbraithian these were correct, would seldom, if ever, occur. Yct in fact between a third and a half of all the products put on the market fail to attract a sufficient number of customers and are withdrawn by the sponsoring companies.[7]

Moreover, the very considerable sums of money spent by firms on market research in order to find out what people want in order to provide it suggests that the consumer still decides for himself, and that firms take a more modest view of their powers of persuasing than does Professor Galbraith. Thus, even in the age of the million pound advertising budget, giving the customer what he wants is still deemed necessary.

The virtues of the market were once well known and its workings understood, if not by the general public, at least by the intelligentsia, although this widespread awareness of its achievements and efficiency sensibly stopped short of slavish adherence to market principles in all things.

Today the picture is very different. A large part – perhaps a majority – of the intelligentsia are either ignorant of or hostile to the mechanisms of the market. There are very few contemporary British accounts of how it works and as a result, recent generations have been taught more about the market's alleged defects than its virtues.

Let me try to redress the balance somewhat by explaining how the market co-ordinates the wishes and economic activities of millions of individuals and secondly, how its operations serve as an effective guarantee of our liberties.[8]

In any country literally billions of decisions are taken a day: every time you buy one thing and not another, buy one type of cigarette and not another, buy one tin of goods and not another, a signal is sent down thousands of networks of communication, indicating what the customer has chosen and what he has not. These choices register with the enormous numbers of producers and potential producers of goods and services who are ceaselessly adjusting to people's choices in the endless spontaneous re-deployment of resources in order to meet demand. The motive is not goodwill. The motive is enlightened self-interest. 'It is not' wrote Adam Smith, 'from the benevolence but from the self-interest of the baker that we get our daily bread.'[9]

In a command system it is quite different. Prices are controlled. All the decisions are made: what to produce, at what price, of what quality, for whom, how, when, where, by officials and they cannot conceivably satisfy the infinitely changing choices, fashion, preferences and possibilities.

In contrast to the businessman who survives only if he satisfies the customer, the official does not depend for his living, his security or his career prospects on meeting the public's wishes.

Thus, the self-interest of the businessman is harnessed to the interest of his customer by competition, whereas in the command system the official must merely satisfy those in the political and bureaucratic hierarchy above him if advancement is to be ensured.

One system rewards industry, flair, energy, imagination; the other orthodoxy, sycophancy, caution.

The market system was not invented. It evolved. It encourages the population as producers to serve the interests of the same population as consumers. It leads people, as producers, ceaselessly to struggle to satisfy the changing wishes of people as consumers. Moreover, it simultaneously and spontaneously encourages in every business organisation the need to improve productivity – the key factor which alone is the cause of a rising standard of living. In a market system individuals are constantly seeking to improve their productivity because the pressure of competition and the search for profit forces people in their own interest to find more economic ways of doing what public demand requires to be done.

I may be told that it is better to produce for use than for profit. But that is what the market does. That is its purpose. Businessmen only make profit if they correctly foresee what thousands or millions of individuals will want and arrange for it to be available.

But the system will work with its full beneficial effectiveness only if certain conditions are met. First, there must be active government to ensure competition. Without competition and the risk of bankruptcy, producers could ignore the wishes of consumers. The nationalised industries are not subject to the risk of bankruptcy. This immunity converts them from servants of the public into protection societies – societies for the protection of the interests of their own workers.

Secondly, we must understand the role of the decision-makers: the entrepreneurs, or risk-takers. The market in its constant adjustment to changing public demand is a world of uncertainty. It is the entrepreneur who identifies a demand and subject to competition and within the law, in the hope of profit, seeks to satisfy it. In order to do so, he or she orchestrates skills, machinery, materials, money.

Without entrepreneurs the system will not work.[10] It is not the workers alone – whether they are manual or management workers – who provide goods and services. It is workers mobilized by the entrepreneur.

But there will not be successful entrepreneurs unless there are both substantial rewards for success and sanctions against failure. People are only going to risk money and endure the tensions and anxieties involved if there is hope of substantial reward. The same is true of managers and investors. We must not grudge, as we do now with our vicious taxation, high net rewards. If we continue to do so, we shall not have entrepreneurs in this country: they will emigrate, or they will opt for a more secure existence in one of the bureaucracies.[11]

The uncertainty and the competition that entrepreneurs meet is fierce. One of the outstanding political philosophers of this century has described competition as 'the perennial gale of creative destruction'.[12]

The pressure of competition keeps the entrepreneur serving the public because he can only survive by serving it as well as or better than his rivals. So the system will not work without competition, without entrepreneurs, without rewards and sanctions. And it will not work without profits. Profits earned in competition indicate that the supply of goods and services is provided efficiently and attractively enough for consumers to pay more than their cost. Profits should be hard to earn but respected when earned. In the private sector, investment and growth can only be financed out of profit. Profit is not what is called zero-sum. My profit is not your loss. Everyone gains from the extra efficiency that competition brings.

Profit-making free enterprise is the base on which all our public services rest. Free enterprise provides the exports, visible and invisible, to pay for our imports. Free enterprise provides the earnings and the profits from which most of our taxes to support the public sector come.

The more efficient free enterprise, the higher the earnings it can pay and the larger the tax base. So the public sector utterly depends upon the efficiency of free enterprise. It is no good urging more money for the National Health Service or for education or for whatever cause and at the same time ignoring the conditions necessary to enable the free enterprise sector to flourish.

You may wish to cross-examine me on poverty. I would explain that, if allowed to, the market will provide a constantly rising set of minimum standards – including rising minimum standards of income. I would explain that there is now very little, if any, primary poverty in this country – that is, households with too little income, if reasonably managed, to pay for sufficient necessities, as currently conceived. Some special groups, such as widows and disabled, have too little income in general for their special needs.

But though there is little, if any, primary poverty, there is in this country a substantial amount of secondary poverty: discomfort, shortage and squalor. It exists in homes where there is an inability to put what money there is to good use. The fact is that whether among the elderly or among two-parent or one-parent families there are copers and non-copers. No one knows how in a free society to teach every non-coper how to cope. What is known is that in many cases extra money does not end squalor.

So we have the purpose of raising the minimum income standards: of trying to help the non-copers and, particularly, of providing more help to special groups such as the disabled and widows who could put more money to excellent use.

Where will the extra resources needed come from? They cannot come from the rich. There are not enough of them – after vicious taxation – to rescue the poor. Re-distribution has already gone further than is sensible and now is actually reducing national wealth by discouraging wealth-creators.[13] If every penny above £100 per week income – earned and 'unearned' – were confiscated and redistributed, the net gain per person in the whole population would be under 70p per week. More redistribution certainly cannot raise incomes or benefits.

The fact is that it is only from the increasing efficiency of the free enterprise system that higher wages can be paid out of which the tax base will rise, thus supporting both higher earnings for those at work and more benefits for those who are dependent.

Poverty is relative. As the general standard of living rises so does the definition of poverty. Indeed, by *this* measure poverty will always be with us – in the sense that there will always be some who are relatively poor. We can never in a free society eliminate differences in income. What we seek is a minimum level of income so high that all have choice and plenty. And, as I have argued, the most effective known means of doing that is by allowing free enterprise to operate more effectively. Some say that I advocate a return to *laissez faire*. Of course I do not. No one wants unrestrained *laissez faire*. There must be a framework of laws and taxes and services within which the market system can do its work of raising living standards.[14]

The purpose of laws and taxes should be to encourage people to do in their own interest that which is in the public interest. The purpose of the services should be to provide for people that which they cannot as well provide for themselves. The laws can lay down any restraints that are considered sensible on what can be bought and sold, on the limits of pollution, for example, on the limits of noise, on hours of work, on safety.

In brief, the market system is the greatest generator of national wealth known to mankind: co-ordinating and fulfilling the diverse needs of countless individuals in a way which no human mind or minds could even comprehend, without coercion, without direction, without bureaucratic interference.

But the market order does not only more effectively than any other system, serve our interests as producers and consumers. It also sustains our freedoms.

Consider for a moment the position of five key figures in any society: the artist, the writer, the reformer, the critic and the inventor. These are the types of individuals who can change a society's attitude. Each of these needs some resources at the start, to support him while he is gathering and shaping his materials and developing his work to a point where he is self-sufficient. The support is needed before he is successful or well-known. In a command society where virtually all wealth is owned by the state, such support can only be sought from officials. There is no widespread ownership of money. There are no independent businesses or foundations. It will not necessarily be easy for our critic or our reformer or our artist or our writer or our inventor to get the support he needs from officials, *particularly* if his purpose if critical of the officials or if it is unfamiliar or unfashionable. Suppose you are a prison reformer or one who wishes to change the treatment of mentally handicapped children; suppose you want to publish a book; suppose you want to do some research or publish a pamphlet or to call a meeting or to hire a hall, all of which involves some money; you have to go in front of officials and ask for it. If they are doubtful of your purpose they will not give it to you.

In a free society, it is very different. There are scores of thousands of businesses, large and small. There are hundreds of charitable foundations. There are millions of households in this country each with hundreds of pounds of savings; there are hundreds of thousands of households in this country with thousands of pounds of savings; and there are thousands of households in this country with tens of thousands and more of savings. All this variety gives to any one of our people – artist, writer, critic, reformer, inventor – a range of patrons for support during their formative period. If they cannot get help from a foundation or a firm or a combination of these, then they can go to individuals and groups of individuals.

There are therefore innumerable sources of help for the reformer, the critic, the artist, the writer, the inventor – individuals whose work shapes and improves a society, individuals who are the yeast and the stimulus of a civilised community.

I will give you an example of the link between cultural, political and spiritual freedom and the free enterprise system.

Who is the person who in the last 150 years has most changed the world? Can there be any doubt? You have guessed. It is Karl Marx. Now Karl Marx was expelled from Germany; he was expelled from France, he was expelled from Holland. In each case as a revolutionary. He came to this country as a penniless political refugee – and for 25 years he worked away in the British Museum Reading Room. He wrote *Capital*[15] and he launched the *Communist Manifesto*.

What did he live on? Did he live on supplementary benefit? Did he get a pension from the government? No, he was supported by one of the large number of owners of wealth in a free society.

He was supported for 25 years by a Manchester business family called Engels.[16]

Do you suppose that in a command society a man like Marx, dedicated to revolution, would have been supported in freedom for 25 years? It is only a *free* society that sustain reformers, critics, writers, artists and inventors. That is why decentralized ownership of wealth and decentralised decision-taking – the decentralization which is the essence of the free enterprise system – is absolutely vital to freedom.

You may say that I am being too dramatic in comparing the market system with the command system. You may say that no one is really threatening to impose a command system on us. Well, let us forget the confessed Communists and the unconfessed ones too. I readily accept that many in the Labour party are democrats and certainly do not want a command society. But, as I have tried to explain, the market system will only work properly if it is competitive and profitable and if the entrepreneurs are encouraged to function and if the need for rewards and sanctions for entrepreneurs, managers and investors are all respected.

If socialist/social democrats destroy conditions essential to a flourishing market system, then the capacity of the free enterprise sector to support the public services and to sustain all our freedoms will dwindle. Already we see prosperity and choice being eroded. Unwittingly, social democrats, driven ever leftwards by natural momentum are destroying features such as selectivity in education, freedom of jobs, freedom to price, pay differentials, rewards for success that are essential to the system. We may, therefore arrive at the destruction of the decentralized free enterprise sector *not* by way of a deliberately imposed command system, but through the purblind erosion of all the conditions necessary to enable the free enterprise system to work properly.

That is why it is so important that we understand the market order. Only if we understand it will we nurture it and enable it to do its beneficent work, and only by imparting this knowledge will we discourage the public from acquiescing in its destruction.

I am not saying that the market order is perfect. It is not. But it contains within itself the source of constant improvement. It is a self-improving system. I defend the market order not as perfect but as Churchill defended democracy. 'Democracy' he said, 'is the worst system yet invented by man for his own government – except all others.' And that is how it is with the market society today. It is not perfect, it is by far the best in existence.

Yet, some of you may say, am I really defending a system like free enterprise with so many scandals? Do you think there are no scandals in a socialist or a command society? There will be scandals in any human society but in a free society with a free press many more of them come to light than in a socialist or a command society.

You may ask if I am really ready to defend the profits made from housing? Yes, indeed I am. In fact, I believe that only if we allow housing to be provided once again for profit – rented housing as well as housing for sale – will we offer housing choice to all citizens, whatever their income.

I am assuming that we help the worse-off by negative tax or some such system.

You may question whether I would go so far as to defend profits made from property? Indeed I would. The provision of property is a proper function in a market system. It involves risk and uncertainty and the supply will better match the demand, as in most things, if the decisions are taken by those who stand to gain or to lose in the outcome. What is not defensible is the state of inflation created by governments which allowed property development for a short period to lead too easily to a paper fortune. Many of the paper fortunes made because of inflation have been destroyed since by the bursting of the boom. If there is no inflation, then property profits are just as well earned and deserved as any others.

It is only the market order that really enables people to choose their own life style. With all the choices that the market offers, much work for good pay through to little work, little pay, people are freer to do their own thing than in any other form of society.

Some of you have closed your minds to what I have been saying. Some of you were convinced before I started of the truth of what I have said. Some of you have open minds. I ask those of you with open minds to compare like with like. Do not compare our shop-soiled reality, with all the imperfections that successive governments have imposed upon it, with some blue-print of a Utopia that doesn't exist – and will never exist. Compare like with like. Compare practice with practice. Compare our imperfect reality with the reality of a different system.

Compare the standards of living and the freedom in countries that have adopted the market order, and have adopted it sensibly and effectively, with those that have for fifty or more years had a command system. Go and look at countries like Switzerland, Western Germany, America. Some of them are run by political opponents of mine. But I say to you that the West German Social Democrats understand how to use the free enterprise system for the good of all better, alas, than have the Conservatives sometimes in this country. You will find in West Germany and Switzerland freedom and the rule of law; you will find social services better than ours; you will find a far higher standard of living than here; much wealth, but you will find very little poverty.

Compare the successful market society with its freedom and its prosperity and with practically no poverty, with any society that runs itself on the command basis with little prosperity, much poverty and no freedom and whose citizens have to be kept from leaving the country by minefields and machine guns. These are the real comparisons and they favour the market not the command order.

Bow Group
Norwich
10 July 1976

NOTES

1. March-September 1974.
2. UNCTAD TD/Sug 8/4, 18 October 1973, HMSO.
3. Tom Brown and Geoffrey Newson, 'Can the patient survive?' *Daily Express*, 26 February 1975.
4. *Group Profile,* Trust Houses Forte.
5. *The Affluent Society* (Hamilton, 1958).
6. H. Demsetz, 'Where is the New Industrial State', *Economic Inquiry,* Vol. XII, 1974; G. C. Allen, *Economic Fact and Fantasy* (Institute of Economic Affairs, 1967); Sir Frank McFadzean, *Galbraith and the Planners* (Strathclyde University, 1968).
7. 'A record crop of hopefuls', *Financial Times,* 11 March 1976.
8. Ralph Harris, *Freedom of Choice: Consumers or Conscripts?* (Aims for Freedom and Enterprise, 1976).
9. *An Inquiry into the Nature and Causes of the Wealth of Nations,* Vol 1, page 27 (Clarendon Press, 1976).
10. Octave Gelinier, *The Enterprise Ethic* (Institute of Economic Affairs, 1969).
11. Tom Davies, 'Why these talents are leaving Britain', *Sunday Telegraph,* 25 July 1976.
12. J. A. Schumpeter, *Capitalism, Socialism and Democracy,* (Unwin University Books, 1954).
13. *Estimated Wealth of Individuals in Great Britain,* 1974 (Inland Revenue, 1976).
14. F. A. Hayek, *Law, Legislation and Liberty* (Routledge & Kegan Paul), 1973.
15. J. M. Dent (Everyman's Library, 1975).
16. W. O. Henderson, *The Life of Friedrich Engels* (Hamilton, 1976).

THE HUMANITY OF CAPITALISM

THOSE of us who defend what I have called 'the market system'[1] have been inclined to take certain things for granted. We have spoken of the connection between an economy regulated by a free market and freedom and assumed that the connexion will be obvious once it is stated. But that is a mistake; the convictions we have taken for granted, that in fact most of us in Britain still share, have been lost from sight.

Perhaps we who defend the market system have contributed to this by talking of the 'market mechanism', the 'price mechanism', the 'signalling system'. This talk has obscured the fundamental assumption about human beings on which the defence of a free economy rests. It is the assumption that men are not machines, not instruments or mechanisms serving ends outside themselves, that they are rational ends in themselves. It is the denial of this assumption, the reduction of men to instruments of social engineering that constitutes the essence and real inhumanity of socialism.

The denial of humanity on which socialism rests appears in the socialist insistence on seeing human beings as productive factors, bundles of interests, workers or capitalists, soldiers in a class war, indeed as anything but rational, choice-making beings. The one idea that has been lost and that we affirm is that a man can choose. A human being is not just better than a chimpanzee at getting bananas out of reach. Men can choose not to want the bananas even when they are hungry. Men can choose even to die because they will not be slaves.

This capacity to choose is what we who defend the market economy understand by human rationality. We refuse to reduce men to machines. If we sometimes fall into the language of mechanics, we are using such language as metaphors. We do not suppose that the so-called laws of economics are like Newton's laws. The *laws* of economics are not regularities in inert bodies moved by external forces. They are regularities in the way in which rational beings tend to make choices under certain conditions for certain purposes.[2]

Because men can see and choose alternatives, they can conceive of different ways of living and want to put their ideas into practice. Civilization as we know it is based on a reverence for this capacity of men to understand and choose, to manage their own lives in accordance with the ideas they invent and arrange. This is what we sum up in the phrase 'respect for human dignity'. And wherever the notion of human dignity has flourished, the worth of a man has been understood to depend on his capacity to manage his own life and to respect the efforts of others to do the same, on what we sometimes describe as the ability to be responsible for oneself.

Men who do not understand themselves as rational, responsible makers of themselves cannot care about individuality. Instead they construe any differences among human beings as victimization, and develop a passion for removing all differences. Thus the reduction of men to machines has inspired the current obsession with 'equality'.

We who value human dignity cherish the differences that reflect the freedom of men to fashion their own lives in their own way. We value a market economy under the rule of law, and we value equality before the law above equality of income, because this is the only social arrangement that enables men to associate and to do things together and, yet, to run their own lives. We oppose socialism because it means a government that runs men rather than makes rules for men who run themselves.

We are not opposed to all interference by government, as socialists claim. We do not advocate a free-for-all when we defend a market economy. A belief in letting individuals decide for themselves how to earn and spend their money is not in any way whatsoever a belief in economic or any other kind of anarchy. We have had quite enough of the nonsense conjured up by that unfortunate phrase, *laissez faire*.

Nor do we believe in a 'natural struggle for existence'. It was Herbert Spencer, the mentor of the socialist Beatrice Webb, who saw relations among men in society as a *natural struggle for existence* in which the strong beat up or eat up the weak. But this is nothing like free enterprise as we understand it.

When we oppose the kind of interference that socialists advocate, we are not denying the importance of what governments, and governments alone, can do. We are advocating a particular conception of government as a maker of rules for men who want to fashion their lives for themselves, who may want to make gardens, write poetry, play darts, chat with friends, watch the sunset; in short, not to be mere drones who 'serve the national interest' or 'increase production'.

Socialists tell us that the arrangements that made us efficient in war will make us efficient in peace. The efficiency promoted by a free market is a very different kind of efficiency. A free market economy is efficient at providing what individuals running themselves choose for themselves. That is not what socialists even pretend to want, and that is why they urge us to seek the efficiency we had in war when we are at peace. A socialist economy is a permanent war economy. But we who defend a free market economy distinguish sharply between a government acting as the headquarters of an army and a government acting as a ruler of free men and woman.

The rule of law that governs a market economy does not spew forth directions or orders for how to live or even for how to get rich. It allows men to choose whether they want to try to be rich or to live quietly doing something they like which does not bring or require much money. And this kind of choice we consider intrinsic to preserving human dignity, to a humane life.

This pride in human dignity that lies at the heart of a preference for a free market economy is coupled with the kind of humility that has been taught by the Judeo-Christian religion. This is the humility that comes from recognising that man is not God. Most socialist thinking is based, with varying degrees of self-consciousness and coherence, on the belief that man can escape human limitations. This aspiration to be more than human lies behind the current obsession with security, the difficulty that men now have in accepting risk, uncertainty, failure, disappointment. And this desire to escape from the human condition makes some ready to grasp at the inhumane vision offered by socialism.

What we, who prefer a free market economy, oblige ourselves to remember is that any attempt to relieve the difficulties of human existence by destroying freedom of choice under stable rules, destroys the humanity of men. Those who urge us to try for perfect security, are urging us to pretend to be able to escape from human limitations. It is a road to an inhumane existence.

We, who defend the free market economy, recognise that because men may choose to live differently there are, and always may be, some who prefer not to, or perhaps cannot, make their own lives, those who genuinely wish to escape the risks and uncertainties of being wholly responsible for themselves. To such people we can say that a free society can accommodate within it enclaves of those who prefer the reassuring discipline or comforts of a tight communal life, whether in the form of a commune, a kibbutz, a monastery, an army, or a nursing home.

But the reverse is not true. And that is what we must never forget. Unlike those who want to run us all as parts of an army we, who want to preserve a free economy, will select policies that can accommodate or care for dependent people in such a way that will not punish or destroy independence.

The morality of those who prefer the freedom of choice that a free market economy can give us is the foundation of our civilization. But it is also the most difficult thing about our civilization to understand or explain. It is besides easy to lose. And we have been careless. We must return to securing and enlarging what socialists are bent on destroying: that understanding of human dignity for which Britain used to be admired.[3]

NOTES

1. *Why Britain needs a social market economy* (Centre for Policy Studies, Barry Rose, 1975).
2. F. A. Hayek, *Studies in Philosophy, Politics, and Economics,* chpt. 16 'The Moral Element in Free Enterprise' (University of Chicago Press, 1967).
3. Lord Blake, *Conservation in an Age of Revolution* (Churchill Press, 1976).

EQUALITY: AN ARGUMENT AGAINST

ACROSS a wide spread of intellectual opinion income equality is accepted as a noble and beneficent objective – and policies to move towards it are recommended and even adopted.

People of goodwill have been manipulated into confusing the ideals of eliminating poverty and of raising living standards with egalitarianism.[1] I shall argue that we can and should eliminate poverty, in the sense of inadequate income for decent choice, but that the pursuit of equality, far from achieving that purpose, will actually increase poverty and install tyranny. If these views seem shocking, that is merely the parochialism of the post-war Western world. To earlier observers they would have seemed self-evident.[2]

I am not arguing against some kinds of equality: equality before the law and equality of opportunity are both objectives which we should certainly aim, so far as practicable, increasingly to achieve. They both enhance freedom. It is the pursuit of equality of income which endangers freedom, prosperity, and the prospects for eliminating poverty.

Of course there is little *primary* poverty in Britain today but there is a great deal of *secondary* poverty – mismanagement of income potentially enough for a modest standard of life. Then, there are large numbers of people, managing their incomes skilfully, who are, if not poor, then very hard-pressed indeed; and whole groups like the disabled, widows and some one-parent households who, however well they manage, have special needs which are not yet adequately met.

Now while no society can eliminate every case of poverty – because some result from, say, gross mismanagement or alcoholism – we should aim to eliminate poverty as such – and we should be able to do it, provided only that we do not follow egalitarianism, the endless pursuit by redistribution of more and more nearly equal incomes.

For the total wealth that a society has is not to be taken for granted nor will it necessarily grow. Our national income depends in a highly competitive world upon our performance – as farmers, manufacturers, providers of services. And that performance depends upon the enterprise, judgment, initiative, effort, skills of millions of individuals – making decisions, taking risks, investing effort, imagination, cooperation, money.

An egalitarian policy squeezing differentials, high direct taxation on nearly all income levels, discouraging capital accumulation and transmission, narrowing the gap between the incomes of successful and unsuccessful, will discourage wealth-creators.[3]

It is no good pretending that the crucial decision-makers can be replaced by public officials. No civil servant, however clever, can respond centrally nearly as sensitively or effectively to the endlessly shifting changes of home and world demand and supply as individuals do, whose careers, families and savings depend upon their being right more often than wrong in judging the market.

The combined effect of lack of the incentive of private ownership and of bureaucratic control explains why a country as rich in resources as Russia is so often on the verge of famine, and has to buy wheat from America whose capitalist system they continue to mock – with a straight face.

I am not saying that there was no scope for some redistribution. To pay for government spending and to help those who need help the better-off should contribute more than those with lower incomes. But government spending is too high,[4] and the progression of direct taxation is too steep.[5] The combined result is that we have in Britain long passed the point where redistribution helps the poor – or anyone else except the increasing number of officials employed on increasingly complex tax and benefit systems.

The marginal rate of tax is resented at almost every income level as discouragingly high, and more and more of those talented people who can create jobs and prosperity are opting out or emigrating.

And yet the talk continues to be of still more redistribution. There is scarcely anything left to redistribute. Redistribution has already gone so far that if all net income – that is, income after tax – above £100 per week were confiscated and redistributed, the benefit would be about 70p a week per head. Even if redistributed only to those with below average earnings, there would not be enough to make a significant difference – and the loss of wealth-creating and necessary skills would grow to a flood. 'You do not', as Lincoln said 'make the poor richer by making the rich poorer'.[6] Besides, the concept of equality of incomes is unrealistic; incomes would never stay equal – except in the graveyard. People differ in their capacity to retain that which they have; to put it crudely: equal at dawn; unequal at dusk.

Moreover the working of a free economy depends upon differentials at every level. Differentials attract people to jobs where labour is scarce; they make long training worthwhile; they recognise effectiveness, hard work, long work, skilled work and responsibility. Abolish them, and the supply of labour for cosy jobs will outrun demand, while difficult, dangerous or unpleasant jobs will be unfilled. How many would rush to endure the rigours and dangers of an oil-rig for the pay of a postman?

If rates of pay do not recognize the diverse character of jobs, it is unlikely that all jobs would be filled voluntarily. Direction of labour would be needed.

The more government levels people and incomes down – by discouraging enterprise and initiative and squeezing differentials – the less productive the economy will be and the less income there will be for everyone, including those who need help.

It is no use imagining that we would be better off with a smaller national income equally shared, and do without the wealth-creators. If we discourage enterprise we shall rapidly descend to a national income far too small to maintain anything like our present standard of living, let alone improve the conditions of those who need more.

Egalitarians should face the fact that equality and prosperity are incompatible. And anyway, people do not want equality. People want more – for themselves and for others. But equality, and even any imposed approach to equality, is the enemy of more. It is not only I, a Tory, who say this. Dubcek asserted in the April 1968 Czechoslovak Communist Manifesto

> I think that the pursuit of egalitarianism is the most important obstacle to higher living standards. Egalitarianism encourages the lazy and the passive at the expense of the dedicated and the diligent.

We shall do better for all, including those now poor or hard-pressed, with a market economy precisely because the inequality of rewards and benefits involved will create greater wealth, which is bound to raise general living standards and can be used to increase social benefits for those who need help.

We *can* eliminate general poverty – but only by a free market economy and by ways which do not destroy the incentives necessary for the market system to work effectively. Less government spending, lower direct taxation, competition and some form of reverse or negative tax or tax credit system. These are the instruments for increasing prosperity and eliminating poverty.[7]

The inequality of rewards by which a market economy functions is not unjust. Most people accept that there should be a connection between the effectiveness of performance, within the law and subject to competition, and the reward.[8]

And most people want to give their children a good start in life. If we stunt inheritance we will discourage some for whom transmitting capital to their children is a motive, and we will make a one-generation society, consuming and not creating wealth.

Besides, there are achievements – farms, collections, private businesses, family houses, for instance – that may flourish best for varying lengths of time in successive generations of a single family. Such achievements enrich life widely; whom will their elimination benefit?

Egalitarianism destroys not only prosperity but freedom and culture. The fewer the individuals with independent resources, the greater the dominance of government. Moreover real freedom – in religion, in politics, in art, in enterprise – depends upon there being many possible sources of financial support. If government becomes the only patron, then freedom – and quality – will die.

The man who has most changed the modern world, Karl Marx, could never have written his explosive works but for a sustained subsidy from Engels, one of the myriad of independent decision-makers that a market society creates.

These independent decision-makers with funds of their own – rich individuals, businesses, charities, groups of average not-rich people – are potential sources of support for variety, innovation and spontaneity – in living, in art, in science, in enterprise, in social reform, in recreation and sport. The state should not be the only patron, for fear that, as in Russia, artists, businessmen, potential critics and reformers will be forced in order to survive to conform to the state's taste or requirements. Many social reforms, many innovations now taken for granted, much art were only made possible by initiative, support, patronage on the part of people and firms with resources.

While explaining that inequality is indispensable to freedom, to prosperity, to art and to the elimination of poverty, the champion of the market order does not have to endorse every degree of inequality. To advocate a free market and the necessary differentials is certainly compatible with redistribution of income to those who temporarily or permanently cannot provide for themselves. Indeed, inequality and the high levels of income that a free economy generates make generous help practicable and raises the standard of living and minimum levels of income.

We who favour a free market economy insist on a safety net to support those who for one reason or another cannot support themselves. But we seek a safety net that will promote rather than diminish peoples' capacity to live as they individually choose: an aid to self-reliance rather than an invitation to apathy. That is why a tax-credit or a reverse tax system is an important aim.[9]

Suppose, however, to return to equality, that incomes were equalised. Would that satisfy the egalitarians? No. The zeal for levelling would shift from economic to other targets. We have already seen freedom in medicine attacked.[10] Already educational practice attempts to prevent differences of talent and aptitude being evaluated and developed. How closely, I wonder, would we come to the *alpha* or *beta* plastic surgery faces – awarded by government for political conformity – in L. P. Hartley's 1984 nightmare *Facial Justice*.

Nor should we ignore the attitudes and motives that nourish egalitarian politics – pursuit of power, envy of those who are different, passion for domination over a battery-hen society – all adding up to a hatred of diversity. Of such motives are tyrants made.

And it is only a small minority that believes in equality and an even smaller minority that wants to impose it. The majority don't want equality. They want more for themselves and for others. Quality and quantity matter more to most people than equality. Yet the pursuit of equality will destroy the chance of more by damaging the springs of wealth-creation. Making the rich poorer does not make the poor richer, but it does make the state stronger – and it does increase the power of officials and politicians, power more menacing, more permanent and less useful than market power within the rule of law. Inequality of income can only be eliminated at the cost of freedom. The pursuit of income equality will turn this country into a totalitarian slum.

NOTES

1. David Bull (Ed.), *Family Poverty; Programme for the Seventies* (Duckworth, 1971); Ken Coates and Richard Silburn, *Poverty: The Forgotten Englishmen* (Penguin, 1970).
2. Samuel Smiles, *Self-Help* (John Murray, 1959).
3. Tom Davies, 'Why these talents are leaving Britain', *Sunday Telegraph*, 25 July 1976; Melanie Phillips, 'Who goes where?', *New Society*, 9 September 1976.
4. 63 per cent of GNP, *National Income and Expenditure* 1967-1975, '*Blue Book*', HMSO, 1976.
5. Robert Heller, *The Naked Investor* (Weidenfeld & Nicolson, 1976).
6. Attributed to Lincoln but was in fact William Boetcker, *The Industrial Decalogue,* 1811.
7. Arthur Seldon (Ed.), *Policy for Poverty* (Institute of Economic Affairs, 1970).
8. H. B. Acton, *The Morals of Markets* '(Longman, 1971); *Why Britain needs a Social Market Economy* (Centre for Policy Studies, 1975).
9. *Select Committee on Tax Credit*, Vol. I, II, III, HMSO, 1973; Milton Friedman, 'Social Security and Welfare', *An Economist's Protest* (Thomas Horton, 1972); *Policy for Poverty*, op. cit.
10. *Hospital Services Bill*, 223, HMSO 1976.
11. Consultative Document to abolish selection for secondary education, Department of Education, September 1975; Education Bill, (146), HMSO, 1976.